Social Reform Movements to Protect
America's Vulnerable 1830–1940

Women & Children
First

*Edited by David J. Rothman and
Sheila M. Rothman*

A Garland Series

SEX IN INDUSTRY: A PLEA FOR THE WORKING GIRL

Azel Ames, Jr.

Garland Publishing, Inc.
New York & London
1986

For a complete list of the titles in this series
see the final pages of this volume.

This facsimile has been made from a copy in
the Yale University Library.

Library of Congress Cataloging-in-Publication Data

Ames, Azel.
  Sex in industry.

  (Women & children first)
  Reprint. Originally published: Boston : J.R. Osgood,
1875.
  1. Women—Employment—United States. 2. Women—
Health and hygiene—United States. I. Title.
II. Series.
HD6027.2.U6A44 1986   363.1′1′088042   86-7523
ISBN 0-8240-7650-8 (alk. paper)

The volumes in this series are printed on
acid-free, 250-year-life paper.

Printed in the United States of America

SEX IN INDUSTRY:

A PLEA FOR THE WORKING-GIRL.

BY

AZEL AMES, JR., M.D.,

MEMBER MASSACHUSETTS MEDICAL SOCIETY, HONORARY MEMBER
CALIFORNIA MEDICAL SOCIETY, SPECIAL COMMISSIONER
OF INVESTIGATION MASSACHUSETTS BUREAU
OF STATISTICS OF LABOR, ETC.

BOSTON:
JAMES R. OSGOOD AND COMPANY,
(LATE TICKNOR & FIELDS, AND FIELDS, OSGOOD, & CO.)
1875.

COPYRIGHT, 1875,
BY AZEL AMES, JR.

BOSTON:
STEREOTYPED AND PRINTED BY
RAND, AVERY, & CO.

PREFACE.

SOME two years since, having been commissioned by the chief of the Bureau of Statistics of Labor of this Commonwealth, to make certain inquiries as to the conditions of homes and employments of working-people whereby their health might be unfavorably affected, I had my attention called, while visiting a factory near my home, to the marvellous rapidity of the digital manipulations required by the processes of a light manufacture conducted by girls. A reflection upon the possible physiological tendencies of such extreme celerity opened a wide door of inquisitive thought; and the interest thus awakened, heightened by the immediately subsequent appearance of Prof. Edward H. Clarke's "Sex in Education," which contained much bearing directly upon the subject, stimulated a wider study of the true relations sex sustains to industry.

PREFACE.

The very considerable effort involved in such further inquiry was undertaken, with many misgivings, for the Bureau referred to ; and its results have appeared in part in its annual report for the current year. The earnest interest and encouragement of Hon. Carroll D. Wright, chief of the Bureau, who from the first has manifested a deep concern in the investigation of the subject, and the more than generous co-operation of Prof. Clarke, have prompted this attempt to place in a form for more general consideration the facts thus obtained on this subject of daily-increasing importance. I have made free use of the wisdom and experience of others throughout this little monograph, believing that the testimony of many strong ones is better than the assertion of a single observer, which, however careful and veracious, taken alone, might be deemed the overexpression of an enthusiast or specialist. I have not hesitated to speak with directness, or to call things by their right names, believing the cause of truth to be best served thereby. That the subject is full of difficulties, the most casual thinker cannot but perceive. In approaching them I have endeavored to keep both the present and future in view, woman's material and spiritual worth, her enforced position, and her true intent. I shall be more than compensated for whatever of time and labor I have expended, if my rushlight shall have discovered any path that shall lead into broader day. Of my inability to deal with so broad a subject, except in the most ephemeral way, and the many evidences of this that this little volume contains, I am well aware. I have made no attempt at assuming Saul's armor, and shall be amply compensated if any of "the smooth stones from the brook," I have thrown from a novice's sling, may have found a vulnerable point in a giant wrong.

WAKEFIELD, April, 1875.

CONTENTS.

PART I.
Introductory 9

PART II.
Objective 33

PART III.
Suggestive 128

"That all our knowledge begins with experience, there can be no doubt."

KANT.

"The end of the state is not merely to live, but to live nobly."
ARISTOTLE: *Politics*, I., 2.

"It is only by labor that thought can be made healthy, and only by thought that labor can be made happy; and the two cannot be separated with impunity."

RUSKIN.

"Women will find their place; and it will neither be that in which they have been held, nor that to which some of them aspire. Nature's old Salic law will not be repealed; and no change of dynasty will be effected."

HUXLEY.

SEX IN INDUSTRY.

PART I.

INTRODUCTORY.

"For this the worth of woman shows on every peopled shore:
Ever as man in wisdom grows, he honors her the more."
ELLIOTT.

MAN, except in the savage state, is a working animal. Even the pre-historic individual erected unwittingly the monuments of his industry, and fidelity to type.

Woman has been, in all time, man's companion and helper; his relation to intelligence determining always the degree of hardship in her toil. Degraded with the savage, lightened in her burdens and raised to higher dignities with each step of man's advance, the lines of Elliott express an apothegm.

Always a collaborator, but assuming new importance as the nature of her true value unfolded, woman's promotion with each added civilization has been toward equal, and in some respects even special partnership in the work of life. Dowered by God with equality of mental scope with man, unlimited like him in her possibilities of attainment, the sole imperative difference in woman, which insists on full and perpetual recognition, is her peculiar sexual principle, — her physiological dissimilarity, — at once her title to complemental rights, her glory, and her opportunity.

But woman, elevated by the advances of civilization, could not escape participation in its incident evils. These have assailed the very citadel of her strength. Imaginary wants have exacted from her an exhausting tribute; and delusions as wild as those of

"The crazy Queen of Lebanon"

have caused her to build from the pure gold of her possessions and privileges an altar to

INTRODUCTORY. 11

false gods. Seeking for her sex distinctive honors, she has proposed to give up for them that which alone could insure their possession. Extremes meet. The demands of savage barbarity held woman in an unsexing servitude. The abnormities of our civilization are demanding anew of woman a kind and degree of labor similarly militant against sex.

Whether it comes from barbarity, or has its origin in false ambitions or disarranged economy, the result is the same against woman, and her highest work in the world, — the perpetuation and ennobling of her race.

The errors of ambition, the ignoring of sexual endowments in the search for attainments and distinction, lie chiefly within the realm of mental effort, — the work of education. The undue burdens imposed upon the sex by the disarrangement of economic forces in society deal mostly with bodily employ, — the domain of industry. Both, however, call with varying degrees upon the same organs;

both preying especially upon the sexual principle and its designed results.*

The physiological characteristics and requirements of the forming female have been so adequately stated by recent writers † in reference to mental hygiene, and are now so generally familiar, that it is not necessary that they should be re-stated here.

An inimical influence upon brain or lower organ, that has its origin in education, is equally inimical if it occur identically in industry. That such identity does occur, and that industry presents in addition its own peculiar phases of sexual unfriendliness, it will be my effort to show.

---

* "Woman, in the interest of the race, is dowered with a set of organs peculiar to herself, whose complexity, delicacy, sympathies, and force are among the marvels of creation. If properly nurtured and cared for, they are a source of strength and power to her : if neglected and mismanaged, they retaliate upon their possessor with weakness and disease, as well of the mind as of the body." — PROF. EDWARD H. CLARKE: *Sex in Education*, p. 33.

† Edward H. Clarke, M.D., Sex in Education; T. A. Gorton, M.D., Principles of Mental Hygiene; Henry Maudsley, M.D., Sex in Mind and Education; Ely Van de Warker; Popular Science Monthly, February, 1875.

INTRODUCTORY.

Prof. Clarke thus reviews the relation of the menstrual function, the salient point of the sexual system, to the health of both student and operative : " The principal organs of elimination, common to both sexes, are the bowels, kidneys, lungs, and skin. A neglect of their functions is punished in each alike. To woman is intrusted the exclusive management of another process of elimination, viz., the catamenial function. This, using the blood for its channel of operation, performs, like the blood, double duty. It is necessary to ovulation, and to the integrity of every part of the reproductive apparatus; it also serves as a means of elimination for the blood itself. A careless management. of this function, at any period of life during its existence, is apt to be followed by consequences that may be serious; but a neglect of it during the epoch of development, that is, from the age of fourteen to eighteen or twenty, not only produces great evil at the time of neglect, but leaves a large legacy of evil to the future. The system is then peculiarly susceptible; and disturbances of the delicate mechanism we are considering, induced during the catamenial weeks of that critical age by constrained positions, muscular effort, brain work, and all forms of mental and physical excitement, germinate a host of ills. Sometimes these causes, which pervade more or less the methods of instruction in our public and private schools, which our social customs ignore, and to which operatives of all sorts pay little heed, produce an excessive performance of the catamenial function; and this is equivalent to a periodical hemorrhage. Sometimes they produce an insufficient performance of it; and this, by closing an avenue of elimination, poisons the blood, and depraves the organization. The host of ills thus induced are known to physicians and to the sufferers as amenorrhea, menorrhagia, dysmenorrhea, hysteria, anemia, chorea, and the like. Some of these fasten themselves on their victim for a lifetime, and some are shaken off. Now and then they lead to an abortion

INTRODUCTORY. 15

of the function, and consequent sterility." *

While pointing out the commonality of effect of "constrained positions, muscular effort, brain-work, and all forms of mental or physical excitement," upon students and operatives in the direction indicated, the same author urges two reasons why female operatives of all sorts are likely to suffer less from persistent work than female students. The first is, that "the female operative of whatever sort has, as a rule, passed through the first critical epoch of woman's life: she has got fairly by it." The second is, "because the operative works her brain less." Though I believe statistics † will warrant the expression that this first conclusion is too inclusive,

---

* Sex in Education, p. 47.

† The United-States census of 1870 gives the total number of females employed in industry between the ages of *ten* and *fifteen* as 191,100 ; total number (of these ages) in manufacturing and mechanical industries, 25,664, or about 13.4 per cent of the whole ; total number females (all ages) employed in all industries, 1,836,288 : showing that 10.4 per cent — i e. 191,000 — of the whole number is under the age of *fifteen.*

the second reason may be debated on several grounds. It is no doubt true that the aggregate of simple cerebration on the part of the female operative is less than the aggregate performed by the female student. But in the intricacy of much modern machinery, the intrinsic mental demands of many processes of employ, and the special mental peculiarities of others, it is obvious that no inconsiderable amount of brain exaction is involved. Again: there are conditions connected with the acts of cerebration in the operative that in and of themselves are potent for evil; as, the monotony, depression, bodily fatigue, and "constrained position," few of which find their counterparts in ordinary student toil. The statistics adduced clearly give a very large per cent as certainly yet under the usual age at which the menstrual function asserts itself, who are employed in the industries of the nation. To this should be added the indefinite, but surely considerable number so employed, who, though over fifteen, cannot be presumed to be confirmed in the

INTRODUCTORY. 17

possession of the "periodic" habit. The exception to a rule is certainly a broad one, that is based on at least fifteen per cent of all the cases involved.

The facts enumerated in regard to the brain-labor of operatives (of which substantial illustration will be given) would indicate, if proven, that, if the labor is absolutely less in the aggregate with the working-girl than with the scholar, its amount is indeed great, and, moreover, is performed under conditions themselves most unfavorable. To these statistics and facts may be added certain other data of kindred significance, bearing upon the main proposition, that the operative suffers less in the vital direction from her employ than the student girl from hers. Dr. Beard, speaking of longevity,* adduces the following reasons for the greater age of brain than muscle workers: "Brain-workers have less *worry*, and more comfort and happiness, than muscle-workers. Brain-workers live

---

* George M. Beard, M.D.: Public Health, p 57.

under better sanitary conditions than muscle-workers. Brain-workers can adapt their labor to their moods and hours, and periods of greatest capacity for labor, better than muscle-workers." The death-rate tables * of three hundred inhabitants of Preston, Eng., one hundred being taken from each of the three classes, — the gentry, tradesmen, and operatives, — give surprising results against the operative class, both as to longevity and youthful deaths.

These and similar observations seem to stimulate at least a doubt whether the dangers to forming woman, conversely of the foregoing proposition, do not equally reside in industry and education. That some of the avenues of industry embrace processes potent in their aggressions against the integrity of female health, with even those of advanced years, has been frequently determined.

But, over and beyond the lines of simi-

---

* See Prin. Mental Hygiene, D. A. Gorton, M.D., p. 116.

INTRODUCTORY. 19

larity in the effects of the influences of the worker and the student, there are clear points of distinction between the relation sex holds to education, and that which it sustains to industry.

The most advanced apostle of a differential education for the sexes demands only, for girls, a modification in method and time; not a substitution of ultimate ends, or rejection of contemplated attainments.

On the contrary, the guardian of the youthful female in her industrial pursuits seeks not only to ameliorate her condition in some, but would bar her altogether from participation in many.

In education, "the question," as Prof. Clarke admirably puts it, "is not, *Shall* woman learn the alphabet? but, *How* shall she learn it?" In industry, the questions, in view of precisely the same physiological facts, are, first, What shall she do, and what not do? and, second, How shall she least harmfully do that which she may undertake?

So far as purely economic and material interests are concerned, it also appears, that if, by the indiscretions of educational methods, the young female sacrifices life or health, the loss, though great, is but that, so far as the state is concerned, of an unproductive unit, and its capacities for increase. If, however, the working-girl is destroyed by her labors, the commonwealth loses both herself as a present integer in the maintenance of society, and her creative possibilities and powers for the future of the race. The student was as yet, in the strict sense, a burden upon the community: the worker was a productive and helpful member of it. The one may have given promise of a life of usefulness: the other had begun it. If an account current, on a purely economic basis, were to be opened between society and these two girls, the student would stand debited with continual outgo, and with nothing to her credit in return: the worker's page would exhibit the cost of maintenance and development to the point when her earning began, and then the credit side would begin to bear figures. But homicidal and suicidal characteristics in the vocations of each have cut short their careers, and closed the account. The balances being struck, it will of course be found, that as an investment, so far as present material interests are concerned, the student has been least profitable: that which was invested is gone. But if future possibilities and expectations could be computed, as longevity is by "life-tables," then the expenditure might stand in the light of a venture whose every promise was satisfactory, but which some unforeseen misfortune rendered a dead loss. Of course it is of paramount importance for the community to prevent a loss, which, if it occur now, is total, but which, averted, by further expenditure and the alchemy of time is transmuted into gain. It is equally clear, that to lose *in toto* an investment that has become a source of revenue, is, so far as present time and economic forces are concerned, a graver loss than the abstraction of that which is still depletory. The value of the one is present and real, that of the other prospective and uncertain.

As our future must be built up out of our present, as the animal must exist for the mental and spiritual to build upon, so far as purely political and social considerations go, the *present loss of the worker is greater.* It is only when we rise to a plane of higher contemplation of life, and view it as more than a social system constituted and ruled only for terrestrial duration, that we obtain a better conception of harmonious possibilities and ends for both student and worker. The power to originate and organize is always greater and more valuable than that of simple execution of details; principles being always higher than their adaptation. A recognition of principles, and the possession of power, are evolved only from breadth of knowledge. Hence there can be little doubt, that were the student and worker both to retain health, and enjoy the normal progress of their several vocations, and eventually find their true place * in the world's work as perpetuators and moulders of it, the student, as a mother and trainer of men, would be most valuable. Carry forward the student and worker to a condition where other standards than those of earth are dominant, and physical bonds are left behind, and the intrinsic individuality of each, being gauged by a supreme wisdom, will find an exact recognition a finite mind could not give.

But the dangers to female life and health from the special ills incident to industrial

---

* "We have been studying woman, in her relation to the subject of this paper (professions and skilled labor), as a sexual being; and, if we continue the study in the same direction, we must arrive at the conclusion that marriage is not an optional matter with her. On the contrary, it is a prime necessity to her normal physical and intellectual life. There is an undercurrent of impulse impelling every healthy woman to marry. That this is a law of her sexual being, we know by the positive evidence of medical men and others. We also know that the married woman exerts a more marked influence upon men, and society in general, than the celibate."—ELY VAN DE WARKER, M.D.: *in Popular Science Monthly, February,* 1875.

pursuits, and their effect upon the public weal, are the present concern.

The results upon the community of the loss of the young female operative have already been shown. Bad as these are,* if the evils of employ break down the health, rather than destroy life, — as is the rule,— a heavier burden is thereby entailed than results from actual death. Years of total invalidism involve both the loss of the individual's production, with its increase, and the production and its increase of those who care for the disabled. Proportionate degrees of dependence

---

* "In Massachusetts, during the seven years 1865 to 1871, 72,727 died in their working period. In the fulness of health and completeness of life, they would have had opportunity of laboring for themselves, their families, and the public, in all 3,606,350 years; but the total of their labors amounted only to 1,681,125 years, leaving a loss of 1,925,224 by their premature deaths. This was an average annual loss of 276,461 years of service and co-operation. Thus it appears that in Massachusetts, one of the most favored States of this country and of the world, those who died within seven years had contributed to the public support less than half -- 46.07 per cent — of what is done in the best conditions of life." — EDWARD JARVIS, M.D.: *Polit. Econ. of Health, Fifth Rep. Mass. Board of Health.*

on others imply proportionate loss. Says Dr. Jarvis, "Nor is the loss by early death all that the commonwealth suffers in diminution of productive power in the period presumably devoted to profitable labor. Even while men and women live they are subject to sickness, which lays a heavy tax on their strength and effectiveness. . . . It is estimated by the English observations and calculations that for every death there are two constantly sick; that is, 730 days' sickness and disability for every death." Reckoning on the basis of calculation furnished by the data of the English "sick-clubs," it is found that there was in the year 1870, among the people of Massachusetts of the working productive age, a total amount of twenty-four thousand five hundred and fifty-four years and eight months' sickness or disability, equivalent to so much loss of labor to the community. The bases on which the English results are made up do not include sickness of less than a week's duration, or any thing less than illness preventing labor:

hence a large total of loss is annually experienced which the above estimates do not include. There are, moreover, certain forms of disease, notably occasioned too by the injurious effects of mental or physical demands upon the sexual peculiarities of young women, which occasion a larger expense for their care than other forms. These are the various types of insanity. Says the author just quoted,* " Under the power of this disease, the sufferers not only cease to be workers, and to contribute to their own support, and that of their families and the state, but are positive burdens for the cost of their sustenance, and the care necessary for them in their wayward impulsiveness, and uncertainty of conduct. In the most favorable condition, the cost of care and sustenance of the insane is greater than that of the sound in mind; and, with most, the expense is very much greater." The cost of efforts at the restoration of the insane is an additional item, and a heavy one, beyond the

---

* Edward Jarvis, M.D., Op. cit. p. 382.

INTRODUCTORY. 27

cost of subsistence, and properly enters into the sum total of the possible burden involved by the loss to effective industry of the working female. There is no lack of evidence going to establish the special tendency of uterine and functional disturbance to produce insanity, and of the predisposition of certain lines of female work to cause these disturbances. It is found that "laborers" hold the second place in numbers among the patients of the Massachusetts insane asylums, and that a large preponderance of these are females. Of these, it is believed that fully five per cent have found the direct or aggravating cause of their insanity * in

* "It is certain, however, that disease of them (the generative organs) may act as a powerful co-operating cause in the production of insanity, without giving rise, so far as we know, to a special group of symptoms. Thus, for example, melancholia distinguishable by no feature from melancholia otherwise caused may be the effect of disease of the uterus. Schröder van der Kolk mentions the case of a woman profoundly melancholic who suffered from *prolapsus uteri*, and in whom the melancholia disappeared when the uterus was returned to the proper place. I have met with one case in which profound melancholia

menstrual disorder or uterine disease (not including the effects of the last climacteric in woman); and it is more than conjectured that a larger familiarity with the phenomena of insanity, and care in examination of insane patients committed to treatment, would establish a considerably increased per cent. As most of the female patients, who find residence in the State institutions for the insane, are those who have followed only industrial pursuits, their disorders, when referable to their avocations, have clearly originated in those of labor. The special tendency to uterine disorders of certain employments will be manifest in their consideration in future pages.

There is still another item in the error account against present customs of employ, which, though not wholly related to physical well-being, both by direct and reflex influence is powerfully operative upon sex, and

---

of ten years' standing disappeared after the removal of a *prolapsus uteri*. Other diseases and displacements of the uterus may act in the same way." — HENRY MAUDSLEY, M.D.: *Body and Mind*, p. 93.

INTRODUCTORY.

its part in the future welfare of society. It has long been recognized, that, for the best good of the individual and posterity, there should be a sound development of body and mind, requiring a pretty definite term for its accomplishment, as a platform on which to rightly pose the special function of sex. A failure to secure this must inevitably militate against physical integrity, and to a great degree affect the moral *status* of the sufferer.

A youthful moral distortion involves inseparable present enmity to right physical and mental development. To this attaches persistent injury of fabric; and, even if the train of physical and social evils incident to prostitution and a life of misery do not follow, there is sure to result a lessened vigor and vitality. The influences that bring about these interchangeable moral and functional perversions are notably abundant in the present " omissions and commissions " of industrial employments. Says Gaskell,* " The

---

* P. GASKELL: The Manufacturing Population of England.

crowding together numbers of the young of both sexes in factories is a prolific source of moral delinquency. The stimulus of a heated atmosphere, the contact of opposite sexes, the example of lasciviousness upon the animal passions, — all have conspired to produce a very early development of sexual appetencies. Indeed, in this respect, the female population engaged in manufactures approximates very closely to that found in tropical climates; puberty, or at least sexual propensities, being attained almost coeval with girlhood. The early age at which sexual development calls into play a crowd of irrepressible sensations, — which, when properly tempered and directed, form the basis of future character, — and the unfavorable circumstances under which this forced development occurs, are in a great measure destructive to the well-being, physical and moral, of those who may well be called its victims." The disregard paid the decencies of life in the location and condition of water-closets, etc.; the laxity with which clothing is worn, and postures are assumed, in the processes of manufacture; the constant association of both sexes in the shoe-shop, the factory, and the store; the temperature, excitement of emulation, etc., — are all actively operative for evil in this direction, in our industrial system. It is an influence whose dangers to society's best interests are co-extensive with its operation.

I have thus reviewed, in an imperfect but suggestive way, the relations of the health of the young female worker, as affected by her vocations, to the welfare of the commonwealth. This review would seem to indicate, that large numbers of her class are of an age at which unfavorable conditions of employ act with dire results against her especial sexual attributes; that severe requirements of brain-exercise, specially inimical to sexual function, are exacted by many processes of industry in which the female is engaged; that there are associate influences of brain-labor in industry of extreme deleterious effect, not occurring with the mental exercises of education; that while with sex in education the effort of the reformer will be to regulate, in industry it will be to prohibit and banish, as well as control; that, so far as purely economic forces are concerned, the loss of the working girl by the errors of employ is greater than that of the student; that the maintenance of broken-down workers is a greater drain upon the community than their actual deaths at an early period; that insanity is a form of disease entailing special burdens on society; and that the unlawful employment of young girls, acting as a stimulant to premature development of the sexual principle, is productive of physical deficiency and immoral tendency, the latter acting reflectively upon the physical forces to their greater detriment. If I have argued correctly, there exists such a sum of antagonism against the foundation necessities of existence, as well demands the earnest attention of state and individual.

PART II.

OBJECTIVE.

"Man is not a system-builder; his loftiest attainment reaches no higher than this: through endeavor, through discipline, through virtue, he may *see* what *is*." — PLATO.

RECOGNIZING the position of woman as a chief factor in all political and social problems, and the necessity to their happiest solution of her most healthful *status*, especial regard has been had to the consideration of employments, which, from their character, might be presumed to affect deleteriously the female operative, and more especially the establishment and normal course of her peculiar sexual functions. The field of inquiry as to the effect of over-mental exertion on the special function of the sex, so vigorously opened by Prof. Clarke, has found many laborers and an abundant harvest. Few, however, have entered the corresponding field of inquiry in industry. Strange as it appears, widely and ably conducted as the investigations of various governments have been into the processes and influences bearing unfavorably upon the health of working-people, with frequent special attention to their results upon child-bearing and nursing women, and (in a general way) upon children of tender years, there seems to have been no effort made by authority, until that of the Massachusetts Bureau of Statistics of Labor in 1874, to determine the far more important, the cardinal relation which labor bears to this essential attribute of the forming woman, on which so certainly hinge all other vital results.

It is curious, in this connection, to note in the otherwise admirable report * made last year to the British Local Government Board " on proposed changes in the hours and ages

---

* Messrs. Bridges and Holmes.

of employment in textile factories," that there is hardly more than a hint in the following questions put by these gentlemen to the medical practitioners of factory districts, of any possibility of injury to the young and maturing female operatives in this most important direction: —

"1. Have you had experience of factory operatives? If so, how long?

"2. Have you formed any opinion whether the factory labor, as now carried on in your district, has any deleterious influence on the health of the operatives? Are there any diseases which you have noticed as being peculiarly prevalent amongst them?

"3. Are there any processes in the manufactures of your district which you believe to be specially injurious to women or children? and, if so, in what way?

"4. Has the labor any tendency to increase the rate of infant mortality? If so, does this depend on the mothers suckling their children imperfectly, or on their working too near their confinement? Do you know how soon married women usually work at the mill before and after delivery?

"5. Do you think that 'short-timers' commence work at too early an age, or that their hours of work are too long?

"6. Do you think the present age of thirteen years too early for a child to commence working 'full time'?

"7. Do you think that the present day's work, ten and a half hours, is too long for young persons or for grown-up women?"

With a careful and highly commendable search for causes of maternal injury and infant mortality, there is here, as elsewhere manifest, a singular neglect of direct and inquisitive attention to the dangers to the basis conditions, on which healthful maternity and infant life depend, and which, moreover, are incident to every one of the sex.

The influences that inhere in special processes or forms of employment, and operate injuriously upon the menstrual function of young females engaged therein, are deserving of, and demand special attention, not less by the gravity than by the extent of their effects.

A process or condition of employ that tends to the prevention or impairment of the normal course of this vital principle in woman involves economic, sanitary, and moral questions of the farthest reach; for, whenever successful in its aggressions, it brings, —

1st. *To individuals suffering thereby*, —

(*a*) Lessened productive labor, and hence lessened comforts of life.
(*b*) Increased expense, and loss of vital force, time, and money.
(*c*) A draft upon previous accumulations, or debt and obligation.
(*d*) As a rule, lessened capacity for future production by labor.
(*e*) Bodily and mental distress, sometimes tending to intemperance and crime, — thus far all results that may be the legacies of several forms of disease, but *specially* resultant on the disturbances in review; while further we have, —
(*f*) Lessened probabilities of maternity or vigorous offspring, with possible resultant loss of social and domestic happiness, and even a worse train of *sequelæ*, including secondary disease, insanity,[*] and death.

---

[*] While the statistics of insanity have been hitherto too loosely collected to give satisfactory and reliable data as to the relation which uterine and menstrual disorders bear to insanity, there is sufficient evidence to show a very close and extensive connection between the two. Dr. Bartlett

2d. *To society it brings,* —

(*a*) Greater burdens, inasmuch as it lays on its members extra care and labor, — in the strict sense unremunerative.

(*b*) Lessened production, present and prospective:
1. By the loss of as much as the disabled laborer would have produced.
2. By the loss of the natural increase of that which would have been produced.
3. By the loss of the production of those required to care for the sick, and its natural increase.
4. By the incapacity to bear a proportionate part, by maternity, in keeping good the strength of the race; or by the expense, loss, and burden involved in the production of non-vigorous and non-productive offspring.*

(*c*) Loss to the general tone and work of society.

---

of the Minnesota Insane Hospital, in analyzing three hundred and sixteen cases of insanity, whose causes he gives, attributes sixty-two, or about twenty per cent, to causes directly connected with uterine disorder. Dr. Eastman of the Worcester (Mass.) asylum, in a review of a hundred and twenty-nine cases, attributes sixteen, or about twelve per cent, to similar causes.

* Says Gail Hamilton, in "Woman's Wrongs," "To give life to a sentient being without being able to make pro-

It hardly seems credible, at first thought, that the class through whom such an aggregate of loss may be, and really is, inflicted upon the state, is composed of the young girls between the ages of eleven and twenty-one, engaged in our industrial pursuits by which their injury is effected. The mortality tables of our cities and manufacturing towns hint at the facts, but rarely include this class under such "causes." Our hospital wards do not often receive them until special agencies of disease have become secondary or general; but their out-patient rooms and the "dispensaries" are familiar

---

vision to turn life to the best account,—to give life, careless whether it will be bale or boon to its recipient,—is the sin of sins. Every other sin mars what it finds: this makes what it mars."

"Physiological inquiries will serve to develop these changes to some extent; facts of observation are likewise in abundance: and both prove that a body worn down and debilitated, although the generative faculty may be uninjured as to intensity in either sex, cannot give the necessary pabulum for the production of a vigorous offspring, endowed with active vitality." — GASKELL: *The Manufacturing Population of England*, p. 169.

to them, and the "corporation" physician and general practitioner are acquainted with their troubles. Profuse, difficult, deficient, or retarded menstruation, anæmia, chlorosis, anasarca and œdema of feet, dyspepsia, pains of back and limbs, nervous headaches, hacking coughs, by and by tubercular symptoms, and more or less early decline, is the usual list and order of complaints that our errors of industrial employ are establishing with this portion of our working-world, and with their results are grafting upon our nationality to its steadily progressive decline and decay.

In the report before quoted,* it is declared, that, —

"Amongst the women of factory operatives, much more than among the general population, derangements of the digestive organs are common; e.g., pyrosis, constipation, vertigo, and headache, generated by neglect of the calls of nature through the early hours of work ; the short intervals at meals ; the eating and

---

* Report on Proposed Changes in Hours and Ages of Employment in Textile Factories.

OBJECTIVE.

drinking of easily prepared foods, as bread, tea, and coffee ; and the neglect of meat and fresh-cooked vegetables. *Other deranged states of a still worse character are present; e.g., leucorrhœa, and too frequent and profuse menstruation;* cases also of displacement, flexions, and versions of the uterus, arising from the constant standing, and the increased heat of and confinement in the mill."

That these ill effects are not confined to factory-operatives alone, but affect the large proportion of females of the industrial class, the physician and the philanthropist have long since discovered. The fact is, moreover, now receiving a general recognition.

What, then, are the errors of employ that entail upon the individual and the community alike these serious results ?

I assume that, —

First is the age at which we permit the young girl to leave a life of animal growth, and become a part of an occupation or a machine.

Second is the disregard (even in defiance of statute) which the managers of our industries exhibit for the cardinal principles of continued prosperity and individual happiness, in the regular and prolonged employ of the plastic and undeveloped forms and powers of these girls of tender years, whose vital functions are as yet incomplete.

Third is their employment in occupations which cannot be undertaken without injury, except by those confirmed in the possession of full strength and capacity.

Fourth is in summoning these girls to a long day of labor, and requiring their unremitting attention to it, under conditions and circumstances radically unfavorable to health.

An analysis of this grouping of causative errors will show, under each division, a demand for the simultaneous exercise of very considerable, often *intense*, activity of bodily and mental forces; and it is believed, that just in proportion as these forces are co-ordinated in occupations and maintained in extreme activity, the impairment and overthrow of the peculiar function of the sex will result. Upon that impairment and overthrow I

OBJECTIVE. 43

desire to fix the observation of all as a prime factor in determining the decline and mortality of young female life, and the multiplied loss consequent thereon. Says Mr. Simon,* medical officer of the Privy Council of Great Britain, —

"The death-rates of the young are, in my opinion, among the most important studies in sanitary science. In the first place, their tender young lives, as compared with the more hardened and acclimatized lives of the adult population, furnish a very sensitive test of sanitary circumstances ; . . . and, secondly, those places where they are most apt to die are, necessarily, the places where survivors are most sickly, and where, if they struggle through a scrofulous childhood to realize an abortive puberty, they beget a sicklier brood than themselves, *even less capable of labor*, and even less susceptible of education. It cannot be too distinctly recognized, that a *high local mortality of youth must almost necessarily denote a high local prevalence of those causes which determine a degeneration of race.*"

An inquiry undertaken some two years since † left little room for doubt as to the

---

* Introduction to Greenhow's Report to General Board of Health, 1858.

† Sanitary Condition Working Classes : Report Mass. Bureau Labor Statistics, 1874.

results of co-ordinated mental and physical activity on the menstrual function. A more recent and extended investigation has confirmed the conviction that the train of evils herein before given as the direct results and *sequelæ* of such functional disturbance are producible in the immature female, and to some extent in the further advanced, —

First, By severe overwork alone.

Second, By severe overwork coupled with innutrition and non-hygienic surroundings, — more rapidly.

Third, By labor requiring great celerity of manipulation coupled with intense concentration and activity of mental forces, — most rapidly, — and especially if under poor nutrition and bad sanitary conditions.

Fourth, Probably, by the secondary effects of diseases engendered or promoted by non-hygienic conditions of labor, as phthisis (consumption), etc.

These causes, then, are direct and secondary, and as ranged under the four divisions or " errors," before declared, may be considered *seriatim*. The *first* of these is —

OBJECTIVE. 45

The age at which we permit the young girl to leave a life of animal growth, and become a part of an occupation or a machine.

"The establishment of the sexual power at puberty, and its extinction with advancing age, both exert important influence on the constitution. At both of these epochs there is an increased liability to disease, and, at the former, a marked increase in the rate of mortality."*

It is evident, that to maintain that condition of life which shall best promote the normal establishment and course of a function so beset with danger, and on whose due exercise so much depends, should be a first concern of all who have any interest in the future welfare of the community. It is

---

* Dr. West on Diseases of Women, p. 18. "It is not enough," says the same author, "to take precautions till menstruation has for the first time occurred : the period for its return should, even in the healthiest girl, be watched for, and all previous precautions should be once more repeated ; and this should be done again and again, until at length the *habit* of regular, healthy menstruation is established. If this be not accomplished during the first few years of womanhood, it will in all probability never be attained."

equally evident, that large numbers of the very class by whom, and toward whom, this care should be exercised, are engaged in employments whose demands and conditions are such as to render them the reverse of favorable circumstances for the true balance of health in this regard. Until this faculty shall have been established and confirmed in its completeness, there can be no moral — there should be no legal — right of a parent or guardian to permit, or of an employer to secure, the labor of the immature frame in occupations that in themselves or their surroundings are inimical to the due development of the individual. If employed, it should be in pursuits free from tendencies to the repression of the sexual principle and the almost purely animal growth which the early years of life seem intended to expressly accomplish. Labors that demand full measures of strength and activity, physical or mental, must properly seek them in those who have passed this climacteric. Dr. Barnes, in his excellent work,* thus clearly states the relation of influence and condition: —

"Many of the factors which account for primitive amenorrhœa (or absence of menstruation) will also induce secondary or accidental amenorrhœa. Thus defective nutrition, unhealthy occupations in crowded ill-ventilated rooms, blood-tainting from exposure to sewage emanations, want of exercise in the open air, which implies privation of the wholesome influences of the sun, — will all prevent the advent of menstruation. It is a matter of observation that girls verging on puberty, sent to boarding-school or into business in large town establishments, commonly fail to menstruate, whilst the function is often accomplished on the return to free life in the holidays, or on return to the country. What is wanted is outdoor exercise, and less rigorous strain upon the mind and body."

In all factory employments, and, indeed, in many others of the lighter and more commercial order, the labors and attention of the employée must be incessant, as well as arduous; and not infrequently the concentrated thought and action of the individual must supplement and be the essential com-

---

* Barnes on Diseases of Women.

plement of the motions of the machine which the operative tends. Even in many of the higher grades of labor in which numbers of young workwomen are engaged, as type-setting, telegraphing, money-changing, etc., the individual becomes almost or wholly subservient to, and absorbed by, the occupation or process to which she is devoted.

Mr. Robinson of Dukinfield, in his report to Messrs. Bridges and Holmes,* says, —

"The injurious element in factory labor is the incessant and increased action of machinery, preventing the body having those brief periods of repose which, if left to itself, it instinctively would have. I attribute the difference in healthy vigor between colliers and mechanics on the one hand, and factory-workers on the other, to the constant demand upon muscular and mental activity made by constant action of the swift machinery.

"Though the thing done is so monotonous and uninteresting, any negligence is fatal to the work, and the attention must be unremitting ; and this call for unremitting attention is increased by the increased

---

* Op. cit. p.

OBJECTIVE. 49

speed of machinery, and the constant demand for increased production.

" The depressing agents upon the physical strength of the operatives are not those which exhaust from the wear and tear of muscular fibre simply, but from loss of nervous energy by perpetual excitement, and from long continuance in overcrowded, ill-ventilated rooms." *

Thousands of children, more than half of them girls, are to-day employed in the various industries of this State, undermining, in a great proportion of cases, that physical vigor which alone will serve as a sound basis for the moral, mental, and material prosperity of a nation.

I have said that the *second* causative error affecting our growing girls in their employments is —

The disregard (even in defiance of the statute) which our managers of industries exhibit for the cardinal principles of continued prosperity and individual happiness, in the regular and prolonged employ of the

---

* Report Sanitary Condition of Leeds, 1842.

plastic and undeveloped forms and powers of these girls of tender years whose vital functions are as yet incomplete.

By far the greater majority of those who are engaged in the lighter labors of manufacturing and commercial interests in our larger cities and towns have not arrived at the age when the law governing such employment releases them from its control; and yet the provisions of the statute in this regard are in large measure utterly ignored, and every section of the State supports industries in the processes of which the law is daily and with unconcern infracted. Probably the first requirement of the law — that " no child under the age of ten years shall be employed in any manufacturing or mechanical establishment within this Commonwealth " — is violated with comparative rarity; but its second and quite as important proviso — " that no child between the ages of ten and fifteen shall be so employed unless he or she has attended some public or private school, under teachers approved by the school committee of the place in which such school is kept, at least three months during the year next preceding such employment, . . . nor shall such employment continue unless such child shall attend school at least three months in each and every year" — is most wilfully disregarded. "No child," says the law, "under the age of fifteen years shall be employed in any manufacturing establishment more than sixty hours in one week. Any owner, agent, superintendent, or overseer of any manufacturing or mechanical establishment who shall knowingly employ, or permit to be employed, any child in violation of this law, and any parent or guardian who allows or consents to such employment, shall, for such offence, forfeit the sum of fifty dollars." There can be no doubt that these latter clauses of the law are most frequently and criminally thrust aside. It is gravely to be regretted that our law has not recognized the established distinction now so generally, as properly and necessarily admitted, as required by the difference in sex, whether in mental or physical labor; has not defined with precision in the law itself, what shall be the interpretation of "knowingly employ;" and has not made definite provision for its rigorous enforcement in every city and town in the Commonwealth. Not that the law is fully adequate to meet the evils pointed out, but that it would, if rightly enforced, go a long way toward the remedy of those evils. While the original error of the law is in admitting to employ at all, in such establishments, girls of such ages, and, as a rule, boys even, and while the change to school occupations — though an undoubted advantage over the hard grind of the factory or even shop life — is but a stepping from one form of concentrated effort to another, even the provisions that do exist in law would lessen, by much, the existing ills if duly recognized or enforced.

It is the *disregard* manifested for the future physical, mental, and moral condition of these important factors in the upbuilding and work of society, and in their individual belongings, that is so unfortunate a feature of the methods of managers; for while want presses, and the " wolf is at the door," present needs will have little thought of future results, and those who employ, or the lawmaking and enforcing power, must be at such time the governing mind.

At the mills in Fall River, Danvers, Fitchburg, Wakefield, Braintree, and other places, there have been employed for years, large numbers of girls and boys, " knowingly," who have not reached the age of fifteen years, and have not a day's or an hour's schooling in the year; and this with the consent of parents and guardians. A further grave defect of the existing law is in its exclusiveness, in that it provides for factory-operatives only. While in certain regards, as in better ventilation and hygienic conditions generally, the lot of the girls and boys of tender years engaged as " cash " carriers, etc., in our large salesrooms and similar establishments, is better than that of factory youth, it is one whose special influences upon young girls can but be injurious in grave measure; for, as I have pointed out, it is the regular and prolonged employ, engaging bodily and mental activity at tension through so long periods of time, that draws upon the energies that should be chiefly employed in maturing and upbuilding the youthful economy. What wonder, that, with these energies sapped by the steady drain of exhausting employment, she should realize the assertion of West,* that "the frail child never passes completely into womanhood, but fades and droops in the transition stage, through which she has not the strength to pass"?

I heartily agree with the prominent Philadelphia physician, who writes as follows of the practice of compelling shop-girls to *stand* behind the counter during all their hours of service: —

"The custom is selfish, cruel, and useless, — selfish on the part of the proprietor, requiring the women to

---

* Op. cit. p. 42.

OBJECTIVE. 55

stand all the time, whether serving customers or not, and this merely that they may appear to be always on the alert to wait on those who call. To stand from seven or eight in the morning to six, eight, or ten o'clock at night, as is the custom at certain stores, with a short time at mid-day for dinner, would weary any *man;* but to exact such service from girls and women is damnable. Their physical powers are, it is well known, much weaker than those of men, at any rate ; and, by their anatomical and physiological peculiarities, they are entirely unfit for bearing this especially severe toil, namely, standing all day long. My professional brethren who practise largely among women are constantly witnessing the evil consequences of this most cruel 'rule of the establishment.'"

My attention was directed, not long since, to a shop on one of the principal thoroughfares of Boston, in whose exceedingly narrow dimensions of only eighteen by forty feet, by eleven in height, heated by a furnace, no less than fourteen young ladies, ranging in age from seventeen to twenty-four, are employed ; obliged by the "rule of the establishment " " always to stand, to dress neatly, and to be absent only half an hour at dinner." Poisoned hourly by the polluted air, suffering from the enforced standing, obliged to dress "neatly" (which was found to mean "showily"), deprived of any opportunity for recuperation in the fresh air (for half an hour barely suffices for dinner), poorly paid, and any loss of time rigorously deducted, it is not to be counted strange if these girls, partaking so continually of physical and moral poison, become both physically and morally unsound. A morality that robs and oppresses does not inculcate a morality to resist temptations to illicit pleasures or deceit, doubtless in some instances impelled to by the deprivations and conditions imposed.

In connection with these errors of standing, etc., Dr. Van de Warker[*] says, —

"The fact that those employments are chosen by women which permit a sitting position is significant in this relation. Woman is badly constructed for the purposes of standing eight or ten hours upon her feet. I do not intend to bring into evidence

---

[*] Ely Van de Warker, M.D., op. cit. p. 461.

the peculiar position and nature of the organs contained in the pelvis ; but to call attention to the peculiar structure of the knee, and the shallowness of the pelvis, and the delicate nature of the foot as part of a sustaining column. The knee-joint of woman is a sexual characteristic. Viewed in front and extended, the joint in but a slight degree interrupts the gradual taper of the thigh into the leg. Viewed in a semiflexed position, the joint forms a smooth ovate spheroid. The reason of this lies in the smallness of the patella in front, and the narrowness of the articular surfaces of the tibia and femur, and which in man form the lateral prominences, and thus is much more perfect as part of a sustaining column than that of woman. The muscles which keep the body fixed upon the thighs in the erect position labor under the disadvantage of shortness of purchase, owing to the short distance, compared to that of man, between the crest of the ilium and the great trochanter of the femur, thus giving to man a much larger purchase in the leverage existing between the trunk and the extremities. Comparatively the foot is less able to sustain weight than that of man, owing to its shortness, and the more delicate structure of the tarsus and metatarsus. I do not think there can be any doubt that women have instinctively avoided some of the skilled labors on anatomical peculiarities."

It will readily be recognized, that the abnormal requirement of prolonged standing is one to which a very large proportion of our working-girls are subject, in a wide range of employment. Both physiological and anatomical considerations cry out against it, and common humanity should prohibit it.

The following illustration, taken from Prof. Clarke,* notes in a marked manner the ill effects of standing, and general error in the conduct of industrial pursuits by our young women: —

"Miss C—— was a bookkeeper in a mercantile house. The length of time she remained in the employ of the house, and its character, are a sufficient guaranty that she did her work well. Like the other clerks, she was at her post, *standing* during business hours, from Monday morning till Saturday night. The female pelvis being wider than that of the male, the weight of the body in the upright posture tends to press the upper extremities out laterally in females more than in males. Hence the former can stand less long with comfort than the latter. Miss C——, however, believed in doing her work in a man's way, infected by the not uncommon notion that womanliness

---

* Op. cit. p. 77.

means manliness. Moreover, she would not, or could not, make any more allowance for the periodicity of her organization than for the shape of her skeleton. When about twenty years of age, perhaps a year or so older, she applied to me for advice in consequence of neuralgia, backache, menorrhagia, leucorrhœa, and general debility. She was anemic, and looked pale, care-worn, and anxious.

"There was no evidence of any local organic affection of the pelvic organs. 'Get a woman's periodical remission from labor, if intermission is impossible, and do your work in a woman's way, not copying a man's fashion, and you will need very little apothecary's stuff,' was the advice she received. 'I *must* go on as I am doing,' was her answer. She tried iron, sitz-baths, and the like : of course they were of no avail. Latterly I have lost sight of her, and, from her appearance at her last visit to me, presume she has gone to a world where backache, and male and female skeletons, are unknown."

NOTE. — "Female clerks in stores strive to emulate the males by unremitting labor, seeking to develop feminine force by masculine methods.

"Female operatives of all sorts, in factories and elsewhere, labor in the same way; and, when the day is done, are as likely to dance half the night, regardless of any pressure upon them of a peculiar function, as their fashionable sisters in the polite world." — PROF. CLARKE, *op. cit.*, p. 130.

The *third* of causative errors we have stated to be —

Their employment in occupations which cannot be undertaken without injury, except by those confirmed in the possession of full strength and capacity.

The consideration of this error, while it embraces the more youthful class to which I have just referred, brings into the foreground those of more advanced years, who, though in part accomplishing the evolutions designed by nature, are as yet insecure in such attributes, and are hence liable to the added dangers incident to their advance. It is not to be hoped for, in this work-a-day world, that we are to be freed from all employments that will fail — with all the alleviations that may be devised — to be divorced from severe mental and bodily energy; neither is it expected, or desirable, that the larger proportion of the class whom we have in consideration — the girls and young women from eleven to twenty-one — should be exempted at once from some form of industrial occupation.

The effort will of necessity be, to establish the right adjustment of forces, all the requirements being considered. The occupations that demand maturity of strength and full possession of functional power for their harmless or least injurious pursuit, are not readily designated; but from investigation it is warrantable to conclude, that those employments which demand extreme mental activity with celerity of movement long continued, involving unremitting attention, condensed thought, and nervous alertness, cannot long be participated in by those whose powers of life are unconfirmed.

Hence the true "division of labor" will be that which delegates processes or occupations requiring the fullest powers of mind and body continuously, to those whose maturity may bear its burdens with least oppression; distributing to the weaker — "to each according to her several ability" — the pursuits which a regard for future weal will not interdict their prosecution of. The true "hours of labor" will be based, so far as sex is concerned, on these considerations; and the true " work of reform " will be such intelligent arrangement of legislation, and its enforcement, and such amelioration of the present attendant ills, as can come only from a just and proper comprehension of these God-created demands of sexual peculiarity.*

To ascertain, as reliably as might be, the effects of the varying characteristics of labor upon the youthful female engaged therein, study has been made of various industries, considering them not as so many trades or vocations simply, but rather as types and expressions of different degrees and kinds of influence exerted thereby; the physical, mental, mento-physical, reciprocal, etc. These inquiries have been especially into the effects of factory employments, type-setting, telegraphy, sewing-machine operation, basket-making, the counting of money, strands, etc., with casual examination into other lines.

---

* "This effort of woman to invade all the higher forms of labor, is a force battling with the established order of sexual relation." — DR. VAN DE WARKER, *op. cit.* p. 470.

OBJECTIVE. 63

Minutes of the inquiry into each are hereinafter given in full.

The *fourth* of these causative errors enumerated is —

In summoning these girls to a long day of labor, and requiring their unremitting attention to it, under conditions and circumstances radically unfavorable to health.

That the hours of labor are long, that the attention to the work in hand must often be most exacting, and that the attendant conditions in which too many of our forms of labor are prosecuted are " only evil, and that continually," are perhaps the most earnestly protested and readily patent of any of the claims put forward by the advocates of the improvement in the conditions of working-people.

The postulate of these advocates * in England, the examination of which created the commission before referred to, was, that "ten hours and a half of monotonous, unceasing labor, even under the most healthy

---
* Bridges and Holmes. Rep., p. 4.

conditions, are said to be a longer time than is consistent with the health of young persons between the ages of thirteen and eighteen, and of women generally, of whatever age."

To this, the rejoinder of the Employers' Association was, "that their bright and healthy appearance is patent to all. Thousands of women are now earning upward of twenty shillings per week; and those of *mature age, whose employment is suited to their strength,* supply no evidence that they cannot with comfort and health work as long hours as men." Even with the very remarkable proviso embraced in this reply, — which I have Italicized, — by investigation, the commission was forced to a conclusion quite the reverse of the assertion, that "their bright and healthy appearance was patent to all;" nor did it conclude, that, in such employment as seemed to be *thought* "suited to their strength, there was no evidence that women cannot with comfort and health work as long as men," though at mature age.

The unremitting attention demanded by certain lines of labor, and commented on as especially deleterious in its influence, I shall consider, together with the non-hygienic surroundings and conditions, in connection with special forms of employ.

An analysis of the four causative errors in the management of industry, which I have assumed to be the chief sources of disturbances peculiar to the working-girl, show, that, under the *first*, we have, —

Youth unequal to the positions occupied in judgment or ability; impairment of animal growth; a constrained condition, as a complemental part of a process or machine. Under the *second*, —

Disregard of ultimate injurious effects on laborers and the community; unbroken application, without vacations, for long terms; depressing and disease-inviting demands on immature vitality. Under the *third*, —

Employ in unsuitable occupations for the condition and strength existing. Under the *fourth*, —

Unduly long hours; concentration of vital energies, involving extreme nerve-tension; unfavorable sanitary conditions in surroundings, and nature of processes.

It will be observed from this analysis, that the various influences under different heads are often exactly identical in their special effects, although arrived at from different initial points, and that each of these special effects is potent in creating the condition under consideration.

We have enumerated four methods whereby the occupations of workwomen may and do bring about the menstrual disturbances and the results we have mentioned, — overwork; overwork, with innutrition and non-sanitary associations; labor conjoining extreme activity of body and mind; and the effects of disease primarily produced by the three foregoing causes. The last of these unqestionably may stand either in the relation of cause or effect, it being beyond doubt that consumption, which produces oftentimes menstrual overthrow in its toil-broken victim, may be and is itself produced by failure of the function in the forming girl.* That one has been the parent of the other, with interchangeable priority, and that both have proceeded from certain evils incident to a life of labor, no observer of the working-women of the land can doubt. " Amenorrhœa (retarded menstruation), especially if attended with chloro-anæmia, is very liable to merge into, *to induce, pulmonary consumption.*" † " Not uncommonly," says Dr. Clapton, " phthisis appears to be developed in consequence of *emansio-mensium;* but phthisis in nearly every case stops menstruation." "With suppressed menstruation,".

---

* "Experience, our only sure guide in medical inquiries, instructs the physician that a diseased condition of the body produces an alteration in the condition of the mind; and that certain emotions of the soul, whether of a pleasurable or painful nature, are universally attended with reciprocal alteration in the bodily functions." — FORBES WINSLOW : *Body and Mind,* p. 153. "Functional derangement and alteration necessarily result from this state of things, leading to disease and change of structure in the organs." — GRAHAM'S *Science of Life,* sec. 305.

* Barnes, op. cit.

says West,* "the one great danger to watch against is the supervention of phthisis."

THE MANUFACTURE OF TEXTILE FABRICS.

The manufacture of textile fabrics, considered as an avenue of production of the several causes of ill health already dwelt upon, may be looked upon as including them all, and hence becomes worthy the closest attention; not only as a source of results so unfortunate, but also as being one of exceeding magnitude, extending its deleterious influence to a wider range than any other equally injurious employ.

While, with exceptions, it may be fairly considered, in the average, as not an extremely laborious employ, either in this country or abroad, for the younger portion of the female operatives employed therein, and in some of its processes in particular, there is a degree of toil disproportionate to the condition and capacity of those engaged; while

---

* Op. cit. p, 45.

the effects of the unremitting and monotonous * character of most of the work can but stand in a direct causative relation to the disturbances and depressions I have pointed out as especially deplorable. It will further be seen, that, in this branch of industry in particular, the special influences that operate for the production and aggravation of pulmonary complaints exist to a degree that obtains in no other. Reviewing the unremitting and monotonous character of factory work, as productive of lessened vigor and vitality, Messrs. Bridges and Holmes * state that, —

"Light though factory labor in almost all its departments unquestionably is, additional leisure of six hours per week would tend to increase the vitality and vigor of the women and children engaged in it. We have already referred more than once to the unremitting and monotonous character of all labor at a machine driven by steam. If the day's work of a

---

* "So a functional disturbance of the cerebrum is often induced by the irregular action of other parts of the nervous system, especially those connected with the reproductive apparatus." — W. B. CARPENTER, M.D: *Mental Physiology*, p. 660.

† Op. cit. p. 60.

housemaid, or even of a charwoman, be closely looked at, and compared with that of an ordinary mill-hand in a card-room or spinning-room, it will be seen that the former, though making greater muscular efforts than are ever exacted from the latter, is yet continually changing both her occupation and her posture, and has very frequent intervals of rest. Work at a machine has inevitably a treadmill character about it. Each step may be easy, but it must be performed at the exact moment, under pain of consequences. In hand-work and house-work there is a certain freedom of doing or of leaving undone. Mill-work must be done as if by clock-work."

The cotton-factory, as well as being the most extensive, is, perhaps, as fair a representative of textile factories as can be given, all conditions considered.

In this department of textile manufactories, it is not probable that purely muscular " overwork," except in very young girls, or in one or two special processes, e.g., " drawing " and " weaving," is a source of any considerable functional injury, ordinarily; but it is interesting to note, that, when it does become so, it is as a result of the grafting on of a species of mental activity, viz., the excitement and spurring involved in the effort of a " piece-worker" to accomplish a certain result, and obtain a proportionate wage.

Contrary to the opinion expressed by Judge Cowley,[*] that "it can hardly be said that piece-workers' health is either better or worse than the health of day-workers," inquiries the present year, both within the mills and of physicians in factory localities, lead to the conclusion, that the piece-workers do suffer, both in general and special disturbance, to a greater degree than day-workers. Inquiry of a distinguished physician who has enjoyed a large practice in one of the principal cotton-factory cities of the State, and who is noted for his exactness in method and record, brought out the fact, as established by his private and hospital records, that nearly a third more came under his professional observation from the piece-workers than from the day-workers. An inquiry after those who had been counted the

---

[*] Rep. Mass. Bureau Statistics of Labor, 1873, p. 282.

ablest workers in the mills through a period of years, and had made largest wages, established the facts that they were piece-workers, and that most of them had broken down in health, and had been obliged to abandon the work.

Nerved by the ambition to be accounted "a smart girl," and with the incentive of gain before her, it is easy to understand how the female operative will attempt a degree of effort that is inevitably "a note given on time," to be paid at maturity, at an usurious rate, from the vital forces of her economy.

"It would seem to be as easy to goad women, as it would be difficult to goad men, into doing the greatest amount of piece-work in a given time. The admiration of their companions, and the approbation of the overlooker, appear to be at least as powerful inducements as the increase of their wages. A woman who can mind four looms without an assistant has attained a certain position, and is an object of attention. 'Hoo's a four-loomer, hoo's like to be wed,' will be commonly remarked of such a one."*

---

* Bridges and Holmes, Op. Cit. p. 20. I am glad to believe that nowhere in this country does the wretched

In the special processes alluded to, "drawing" and "weaving," it may well be doubted if a labor, which, as in the first, requires the constant removal of the cans (or boxes) to and from the machines, weighing when full from sixteen to eighteen pounds (upward of nine hundred cans passing through the hands of each female in a day), is not a species of overwork in itself, that, so continuously plied, must result in injury. In "weaving" and in "spinning" both, it has been a common mistake to employ girls whose ages could but be associated with sexual insecurity that should of itself class this employment for them as overwork.

"Where labor is also prejudicial," says Dr. Baker,* of Leeds, "there needs not miasm, and want of ventilation, to accelerate its con-

---

and abusive custom exist of determining the pay of the "overlooker," or foreman, of a room by the earnings of those under him,—a system which, wherever practised, is accompanied by the most brutal goading to over-labor, productive beyond escape of a host of evils to health.

* Report on Leeds, in Reports on Sanitary Condition of Laborers, Population England and Wales, 1842.

sequences; and there is no doubt but that atmospheric influences have a preponderating effect on many occupations: *they germinate and ripen the seed which labor has sown.*"

Judge Cowley bears testimony that "the special diseases incident to factory life are lung diseases and 'female debility.'"

Dr. H. Browne of Manchester, Eng., states that "diseases of the digestive and respiratory mucous membranes are not quite *twice* as frequent in the factory-workers who attend the infirmary as out-patients, as in the remaining out-patients of all classes and both sexes."

The Massachusetts State Board of Health has undertaken an inquiry into the mortality of factory-operatives within their jurisdiction. An analysis of the replies received by this board[*] to its queries establishes the fact that the employés of cotton-factories suffer a disproportionate death-rate. The registra-

---

[*] Second Annual Report Massachusetts State Board of Health, p. 414.

tion reports of Massachusetts for the last nine years also show, that, in the large manufacturing towns, the death-rate from diseases presumably incident to such employ exceeds that of other towns of similar population. We have, therefore, the testimony of our own and foreign observations, to the existence of results which we have come to recognize as associated with special causes, more especially overwork coupled with innutrition and non-sanitary surroundings.

Notwithstanding the great improvements which the past few years have made in cotton-machinery, and the processes of labor in cotton-factories, the following comprehensive statement of a German writer * still too correctly depicts the effects of labor in the dust, etc., of such factories.

"Soon after entrance into the workshop, the workman perceives it (the dust) in a most unpleasant way. In those who are unaccustomed to it, it causes continual tickling in the throat, which incites

---

* Dr. Ludwig von Hirt: Krankhirten der Arbeiter, Breslau, 1871.

hard coughing and occasionally whitish expectoration. In the first year of work, the operative suffers constantly from bronchial catarrh; and a considerable proportion of those who come to this occupation from rural districts abandon it, even though they may be only sufferers from constant catarrh, without other worse symptoms.

"If, however, they persevere in this occupation, more important symptoms supervene, sometimes soon, often after a year of work, such as cough with pectoral pain, marked anæmia, obstinate debility, and loss of appetite. White viscid sputa is now expectorated with difficulty, and shows under the microscope cotton-fibres for several hours after quitting the factory. Marked emaciation, sometimes — but rarely — profuse diarrhœa, deprives the operator of his strength, and compels him to leave his work, and betake himself to his home or to the hospital.

"These, of course, are the most unfavorable, and happily not the most frequent cases. But people very often go on coughing their whole life long, and die at an advanced age. . . . Sickly people, especially those liable to pulmonary affections, do not bear up long. *The most unfavorable cases are usually found among women;* and in a factory of three hundred or four hundred operatives, there will generally be found two or three cases of this kind every year. Other diseases of not infrequent occurrence are phthisis, acute pneumonia, and, as has been already remarked, chronic catarrh."

The processes of "carding" and "stripping," even since the introduction of Wellman's patent stripper, etc., still fill the air with innumerable particles of dust which penetrate everywhere, and, in some mills, in a few minutes sufficiently coat a smooth plate of metal to permit the finger to make marks thereon; while a sunbeam discloses the extent to which the atmosphere breathed by operatives is charged with the foreign substances.*

A careful inspection of a very large number of factories has established as the chief non-hygienic conditions, the excess of flying dust, or "fluff;" the extreme heat maintained in all departments; the uncomfortable and unhealthful humidity, particularly of

---

* Dr. Horatio Bridge of New-York City, a classmate, has recently published an admirable translation of the work of Dr. Gottlieb Merkel of Nuremberg, on *diseases caused by the inhalation of dust*. New-York Medical Record, 1874.

the weaving-rooms, from steam; the special irritations from the operation of "stripping," and perhaps, to some extent, from that of "grinding;" the irritation and noxious influence consequent on the "sizing" employed; and the specially evil effects of foul privies.

When to these are added the ills that result from insufficient, unfit, and hastily devoured food, and wet clothing, from the long standing, reaching, and lifting (as of heavy beams), and the depressing tendencies of the monotony and unrelenting exactions of the processes themselves, we have a sum total of causes quite sufficient to wage successful war upon the general health, and to break down and overthrow the special forces Nature would fain establish in those subjected to these repressing agencies.

Of several of these agencies enumerated, the English commission reported last year, to Parliament, as follows: —

"As to ventilation, in almost all cases it was extremely bad, and in a large number of instances there was none whatever. . . . The heat is kept up by steam-pipes, and obvious motives of economy dictate that as little as possible of it shall be lost by open windows. . . . In most of the spinning-rooms there are one or more privies, usually of very rude construction, and almost always opening directly into the room, with very inadequate apertures to the outside air. The soil falls down a large untrapped pipe, which is flushed often or seldom, according to the varying attention given it."

This is a picture that would be entirely correct of many factories to-day in this Commonwealth, though I am glad to believe that a marked improvement in these regards has characterized nearly all larger factories, and some of the smaller.

Wherever the manifestly injurious influences I have mentioned are present, there cannot fail to be both physical and mental impairment, ill suited to sustain or to resist the further encroachments of the demand made by certain of the processes of factory labor for alert co-operation of mind and body.

Exhibiting, as it does, so great a variety and grave a degree of devitalizing power upon woman, in its concomitants otherwise, it is fortunate that cotton-factory labor necessitates so small an exercise, as it does, of the expressly untoward influence which arises from co-ordinate energy of mind and body.

Whether we agree with Dr. Seguin,* or not, in his view that " co-ordination is no faculty, but a function of every portion of the motor tract of the spinal axis from the origin of the third cerebral nerve down," it is certain, that, operating between mental and physical forces, it has a power for exhaustion not found in the fullest exercise of either alone.

In cotton-manufacture, it is only in the routine work of attendance on machinery which requires the exact adaptation of mind and hand at precise times, that this coeval demand upon thought and its executing power is made ; and here the speed is rarely such, or the concentration so absorbing, as to

---

* An Outline of the Physiology of the Nervous System: E. C. Seguin, M.D. N. Y. Medical Record, Dec. 1, 1874.

prevent some degree of unconscious or "mechanical" response and restful inattention.

The numerous causes provocative of pulmonary disease, which have been cited as existing in factory labor, leave no room for doubt, that the destruction of menstrual power, which so certainly supervenes on the development of phthisis, may readily receive its origin here; while it is equally evident that these causes, if co-operating with those acting directly upon the function itself, can but hasten the result it should be the aim of the employer and the legislator alike to avert.

A searching analysis of the "examination notes" of one hundred and twenty-four mills in the Commonwealth shows to have been specially noticeable for wretched ventilation, sixty; while there were "noted" as observable for overheated rooms (particularly weave-rooms), thirteen; dusty and exceedingly dirty condition, fifteen (from "size" one); bad condition of privies, nearly all;

employment of girls under ten years, eight.*

I pass now to the consideration of several employments, in none of which purely muscular overtaxing occurs, and in which the innutrition and numerous non-hygienic influences inherent in mill-life are principally absent, but in which the most potent of causes of sexual derangement, *simultaneous activity and concentration of mind and body*, is noticeably present. It is observable, moreover, that, in these, the distinctive feature of the corresponding activity in factory labor, viz., monotony and its depression, is lacking; and inasmuch as, despite these advantages, it is found, that, as a whole, this order of labor is far more rapidly and certainly destructive of the normal balance of the sexual principle in women, we must con-

---

* The United-States census of 1870 gives as the total number of girls between the ages of *ten and fifteen* employed in the industries of Massachusetts, 6,299; the larger proportion of whom are, beyond doubt, subject to the evils here enumerated.

clude, that in the greater *rapidity* of effort, physical and mental, involved; in the great increase of *concentration* required ; and in the *contemporary* exercise of the forces brought into play, — the exceeding deterioration must reside.

It is but fair, however, to observe that the class of females engaging in these occupations — all of which require a higher degree of intelligence than most mill-work — is of a more highly-organized character; and, as being of more sensitive fibre, might rationally be expected to sooner exhibit the results of the attrition and wear incident to these pursuits.

TYPE-SETTING.

The setting of types, the labor of the " compositor," as this servant of the public is called, holds a peculiar position in the class of physico-mental activities from the facts that the employment —

May become partially unconscious or " mechanical " labor ;

Is supposed to possess certain dangers of poisoning from the nature of the metal composing the types; and —

Has in the postures necessary, its sedentary character, and the heat at which "composing-rooms" are unavoidably kept, its particular non-hygienic conditions.

It will readily be seen, that a closely attentive activity must be exercised to "follow copy," and accomplish a paying amount of work with sufficient correctness to satisfy employers. There can, of course, in this labor, be no distracting influences; for to "set" type with a remunerative degree of rapidity and correctness (and most type-setters are required to "correct" their own "proofs," or errors), the eye must take in the words of the copy, and their relations to each other, their punctuation and character (whether Italics or other type), and various other details known only to the guild; must transmit the intelligence absorbed by the eye to the hand, and direct it with celerity to that particular one of the compartments in a type "case" which contains the particular type called for, and deftly arrange it "wrong-end first" in the proper relation to its fellows contained in the "composing-stick." To read the copy (often most illegible); to supply or correct punctuation; to determine the type, "spaces," "leads," etc.; to observe the intended sense of the writer; to separate sticky type, "keep them on their feet," place them correctly, duly "spaced" and "leaded," as well as punctuated; keep the place in the copy; and do all these quickly, sometimes with cold hands, and with various interruptions, — it is obvious, is an employment that is most exacting of mental concentration and manipulative rapidity. A good female compositor can "set" and correct thirty thousand ems per week, for which she would receive thirty cents per thousand, although many are employed at a set sum per week, rarely exceeding ten dollars; and at this rate she would be expected to be able to set nearly six thousand ems per day, to accomplish which it will be seen that there must be constant labor of a very rapid character.

As an offset, however, we have the fact, that a considerable portion of the work becomes mechanical, a skilled compositor knowing, without looking, exactly where in her case to find the type wanted; while the placing it in position in the composing-stick correctly is accomplished by the aid of another of those marvellous processes of mental telegraphy with which our daily actions are replete. The type has upon one side a series of "nicks," which being felt by the finger, the brain is informed, and, without the intervention of the eye, the type is turned to the correct position, and set by the re-instructed finger. The wrong-end-first position of the type is, moreover, no impediment to the compositor, who reads "backwards" and "upside-down" as well as other people regularly read from left to right. Hence it is to be considered, that, although an employment of distinctly co-operative physico-mental activity, it is lessened in degree as such by the

OBJECTIVE.

facility with which its processes, in part, become mechanical. It is a question not readily determined, whether or not the pernicious effects of the depressing powers of lead and antimonial poisoning (where they are operative), and of the heat and unhealthy postures mentioned, are the equivalents of the gain derived to the compositor by her power of making the work partially mechanical; and so advantage and disadvantage balance each other, and leave the employment a pure type of its class. An exceedingly interesting feature of type-setting is the fact, that it is understood, by first-class compositors, that the element of memory enters largely into, in fact becomes a governing power in, the occupation, thereby changing the direction and character of the mental concentration. Having read her copy, it is asserted that the compositor, if of good memory, retains the sentence read, in mind, follows copy no more till a fresh sentence is needed, and then concentrates all thought upon retaining the sentence and the point in it, to which work has progressed, leaving the eye free to go with the hand to the case, aiding the correctness and celerity of the latter. It is plain, that, if such is the mental process, the greater the retentive power of memory (largely, of course, a matter of training), the more freely and rapidly the work may go on, the true concentration being upon the two points mentioned; viz., the general retention of the sentence, and the place reached therein by the compositor.

It is proper to note, moreover, in this connection, that a compositor who is quick of perception, and is skilled in grammatical construction, punctuation, etc., is able to perform her work with much less fatigue than one of slower comprehension and less accomplishment. Finding that the foregoing views, as to the part played by memory, and the degree of skill in perception, grammar, etc., were fully recognized, it became a matter of much interest to confirm them by actual experiment and inquiry. A well-established case was found to be familiar to the older compositors, of a compositor who had been an " expert," becoming totally *blind*, but continuing his work by having a boy to read long extracts of his copy to him, his cultivated powers of retention being remarkable; and it was found that his proofs were, in the main, as correct as those of his fellows. Desirous of determining the real force of this claim, a lady compositor was carefully blindfolded; and, the copy being read to her, it was found that the work could undoubtedly be thus performed, though with not quite the same correctness as ordinarily, but more rapidly, and resulting in greater fatigue. The statement of the operator was to the effect, that her whole concentration of mind was upon the two points already mentioned, — the retention of the copy, and her place in it; and this concentration she considered quite equivalent in demand to that required by the slower process of setting with the eyes open, stating that she missed the aid in keeping the place, obtained by the hurried glance upon the state of progress in the composing-stick. Whatever ameliorating circumstances it may possess, in any or all of the ways mentioned, it is evident that type-setting is an employ exacting an unusual degree of mental concentration and energy, with great rapidity of manipulation; and, as such, if previous hypotheses have been correct, cannot fail to have a marked effect upon the health of its female operatives. Let us see how these hypotheses are borne out by the facts, as variously obtained.

Mr. M——, brought up in the business from a boy, now engaged in it for eighteen years, having worked in offices with female compositors ranging from one to twenty in number, and including from two to three hundred in his observation, states, —

"Few girls can continuously set more than five thousand ems per day, while men will set from seven to eight thousand; not because the girl is not quicker in movement and perception, for she *is*, but because she cannot 'stand it,' — she is not strong enough. It seems to be the back that gives out. Girls cannot work more than eight hours, and keep it up : they know it, and they rarely will ; and even this seems to 'pull them down,' so that it is extremely rare that a girl continues more than a few years at the business."

Mr. B——, foreman of a large printing establishment, says, —

"Girls must sit at the 'case.' I never knew but one woman, and she a strong, vigorous Irishwoman of unusual height, who could stand at the case like a man. Female compositors, as a rule, are sickly, suffering much from backache, headache, weak limbs, and general 'female weakness.'"

Mr. D——, the publisher of a well-known periodical, says, —

"I have had hundreds of lady compositors in my employ ; and they all exhibited in a marked manner, both in the way they performed their work and in its results, the difference in physical ability between themselves and men. They cannot endure the prolonged close attention and confinement which is a great part of type-setting. I have few girls with me more than two or three years at a time ; they must have vacations, and they break down in health rapidly. I know no reason why a girl could not set as much type as a man, if she were as strong to endure the demand on mind and body."

Miss J——, a lady compositor, says, —

"We cannot stand at the 'case.' It increases back and head ache, and weakness of limbs, as well as a dragging weight about the hips. I have been at this work five years, but have been frequently obliged to give up for vacations, from peculiar troubles and general debility. I began to menstruate when fourteen; I am now twenty-two. I was well until I had set type a year, when I began to be troubled with difficult periods, and have been, more or less, ever since. When I go away, I get better; but, as often as I return to my work, I am troubled again. Have wholly lost color, and am not nearly as fleshy and heavy as when I began work. I have now a good deal of pain in my chest, and some cough, which increases if I work harder than usual. I am well acquainted with many other lady compositors who suffer as I do."

Miss S——, a lady long in charge of the "composing-room" (female department) of a large printing establishment, testifies, —

"I was myself a compositor, and have had scores of girls under me and with me, many of whom I have known intimately. I have no hesitation in saying that I think I never knew a dozen lady compositors who were 'well.' Their principal troubles are those belonging to the sex, and great pain in back, limbs, and head. Most of those I have known have preferred going into other employments than to continue in the business. Many seem to recover fully after leaving the business; but I have known several who have sickened and died of 'consumption,' and some are always troubled with 'female complaints.' I know a number who have married, and have children, most of them seemingly bright and healthy. Girls cannot stand at the case like men, and ought not to try to work, if it can be helped, at certain periods. I think the heat and ill-ventilation of our rooms is bad for us all."

Dr. G——, a physician in one of the suburbs of Boston, gives his evidence as follows: —

"I have had several cases of menorrhagia (profuse menstruation), a few of retarded or difficult menstruation, and a single case of type-poisoning, in female compositors. They all tell me that the work produces backache and headache, with more or less trouble periodically. The case of poison was an interesting one, and proved itself such conclusively. As often as the girl would leave her work for a time, her unfavorable symptoms would entirely remove : just as soon as she took up the types again, the trouble was renewed. It is an employment requiring so close confinement, and such careful attention, that I am at no loss to understand its effects."

Mr. H——, an employé of the government printing office at Washington, informs us, —

"I have known a good many of our girls in the composing-rooms here in the city; and quite a number that I have known have come here into the work strong and healthy-looking girls, and have gone away in a few years, pale, thin, and sick. I know, from conversation with some of them, that the work upsets them as women, and they cannot continue the work long without suffering. I should say, that perhaps their pleasure-seeking after work — as balls, parties, etc. — has a bad effect too; but all do not follow that course."

Dr. B——, a physician to dispensary patients, says, —

"I have seen quite a number of female type-setters who were suffering from uterine troubles and disturbed menstrual conditions. I think that these, with obstinate constipation, and occasional cystitis (inflammation of bladder), are their chief troubles, beside the ever-present 'headache.' Mind and body are compelled to act so quickly in that work, that I am not surprised at nervous effects, particularly in young women not fully developed."

It will be seen from the foregoing, that the female compositors themselves, their employers and associates, those who superintend them, and their physicians, all agree to the effects of the labor, and the latter recognize the cause. Although subject to modifying, and to a certain degree puzzling, circumstances, there can, apparently, be no doubt of the relation existing between type-setting, as an employment possessing the physico-mental draft, and the conditions found to exist in those devoted to it. Counting it, therefore, as an interesting and conclusive illustration of the physico-mental influence upon the peculiar function of woman, and leaving our suggestions concerning it to a further consideration, we pass to the review of an occupation still more closely a type of concentrated mental and physical co-operation.

TELEGRAPHY.

Those at all familiar with the demands upon the nervous energy and manipulative dexterity required by the processes of telegraphy will not be surprised that the rapidity, readiness of perception and response, sensitiveness to "time," close attention to the "delivery" of the instrument, manual celerity, and often simultaneous action in "receiving," counting, writing, and "checking," are found to exert upon the general and special health of the youthful "lady operator" a most positive and rapidly injurious effect. That it has not more widely attained a reputation as a "non-salubrious" employ, is due to the facts, that those engaged in its most responsible, and therefore most hurtful positions, are with very rare exceptions safely past the forming period, — are confirmed in their possession of womanly attributes; and those of impressible years are usually employed in "branch offices, " etc., places that do not exact that continuity or concentration in their work

OBJECTIVE.

that main offices, etc., must have. These being the facts, it is doubly interesting to find, that, so purely is the occupation one of the physico-mental activity type, that though in the one case the labor is intermittent, and permissive of rest, and in the other the operator has passed the climacteric, the demands for concentration and co-operative alertness are so great, that both suffer in health in a marked and universally recognized manner. It is but fair that the constrained posture, sedentary habit, obstinate and confirmed constipation, and over-heat of the rooms, which very generally affect the operator, should be given due place in the causative effects of this recognized disturbance of health ; but to the character of the work itself is the great proportion of the result due.

While, therefore, this particular avenue of employ cannot be looked upon as one of those affecting, to a wide extent, the peculiar sexual function in forming girls, from the fact that comparatively few such are employed therein, it is of great interest, as establishing in a marked manner the soundness of the principle put forth, that, from a rapid exercise of concentrated mental and physical energy, there occurs the most emphatic effect upon the function in consideration. Wherever young girls are called upon to engage in the full requirements of a busy office, or experience a sudden increase of labor and responsibility, the effect on the economy is immediately apparent, and especially in the direction of the menstrual result, if contemporaneous.

"It is the common thing," says the superintendent of a line, "for young beginners, those promoted to larger offices, and those placed suddenly upon responsible posts, to suffer a degree of physical prostration immediately thereafter; and I have noticed this to be proportionate to the age and nervous habit of the individual." Numerous inquiries of operators, in a score of offices, have produced the unvarying answer to the question, "How long can you stand this employ in a busy office?"—"Not over a year, without a good vacation of at least a month." Indeed, that this is so, the managers of the principal lines seem to recognize, inasmuch as a month's vacation is allowed their " operators " in each year; though it is to be greatly regretted, that, even for sickness, they will make no further allowance, compelling the operator to resign if even a day or two more, however imperatively demanded by illness, is taken.

On being interrogated as to the special causes and effects of prostration in telegraph-offices, the first reply of nearly all young "lady operators," perhaps not unnaturally, is to the effect, that the close confinement, over-heat of rooms, and position, are principally operative; but more direct inquiry, calling out the more active and self-examining thought, invariably produces the reply, that the "nervous debility," "cold feet and hot head," and dizzy headache, make up a good part of the results; while particular inquiry, in a large proportion of cases, establishes the fact, *always*, in the larger offices, that menstruation occurs more frequently than it ought.

When it is known, that, in the average business of a large city office, a " lady operator " often receives a string of messages with the ear, writes them as they come with her right hand, counts them with her eye, checks them with her left hand, and answers her " O. K." to the sender, it will be readily understood that the interplay of nervous influences must be of the most rapid and exhaustive character ; because, however expert the operator may become, she can never become purely automatic: mental *concentration* must be drawn upon to the full. A "lady operator," many years in the business, said to me, —

"I have broken down several times, completely worn out, suffering from sheer nervous debility. I had 'turned of age' safely, and was well in this and every other particular when I entered the office : since I broke down the first time, I have never been 'right,' though much improved when out on my vacations. I could not have continued as long as I have, if it had not been that I have been changed about in small offices, and have been part of the time in charge of rooms."

Another said, —

"Our girls all come to us looking bright, fresh, and ruddy ; but it is not long before they lose color, and strength seems to go with it. While I think it a nice occupation, and better than standing in stores or working in mills, it would be much better if vacations could be better arranged, and the confinement lessened."

Miss ——, for several years in charge of the female department of one of the largest offices in the country, testified, —

"One year is as long as one can work in a busy office without a good vacation. The confined position, constipation, heat, and dizzy headache, I think, are the most noticeable troubles of 'lady operators' who are 'grown up.' The hours are too long for such strained employment. From eight, A.M., to six, P.M., with only an hour for dinner, makes too long a day for the kind of work. I am sorry to say some of our girls eat their lunch in the room, not going out at all. A woman can do as much as a man in this business, and do it as well, but does not get the same pay for it. A skilful 'lady operator' here will sometimes have from two hundred to two hundred and thirty messages a day; *but she could not stand that rate more than a month.* Most of our chief-office 'lady operators' are from twenty-three to twenty-four years old: our youngest is twenty-three. They generally begin to learn from sixteen to eighteen years of age, and *the youngest, of course, feel it most.* I think, that, with those of our age, the chief menstrual trouble is with its occurring too often."

An inquiry of those among female operators who more properly came within the designation of "forming" has developed some curious and interesting results.

Miss C., a "lady operator" nineteen years of age, located at an office in a quiet town on one of our railroad lines, owing to an accident on the line, had her office suddenly besieged for an entire day and into the night, by an unprecedented business, taxing her to the utmost. It occurred just at a "peculiar period:" a complete suppression resulted, and a general prostration ensued, from which she has slowly and imperfectly, as yet, recovered.

On "election night" the demand upon operators is, of course, unusually heavy; and several of the female operators at large centres state, that, for some days after, their sense of debility is great. In two cases the periodicity was notably disturbed by this or any other unusual requirement of the work, just previous to the time of normal recurrence.

It not infrequently happens that sickness of an operator, or other contingency, requires the transfer of a young operator from her usual post to one of greater responsibility and more exacting duties; and in such cases the operators are quite liable to find that a considerable disturbance of their periodical function occurs. Whenever a young operator is transferred to one of the chief offices, especially if a person of nervous temperament, the increased responsibility and nervous agitation (unless a person of unusual confidence and poise) will not infrequently occasion a disturbance of this character more or less prolonged. The weight of evidence would seem to indicate, that, with those of the "forming-period," the result of such influences is to repress and retard; while, with those of maturer years, it is to render more frequent and profuse. It is to be regretted that it is not readily possible to more completely separate the other deleterious influences, as posture, confinement, etc., from the distinct operation of the physico-mental concentration and activity. A review, however, of the foregoing, indicates conclusively that, —

Though the extent of the employ of "forming" girls is not wide, wherever occurring, the results are those declared, and are exactly such as we should expect from the class of influence at work;

That this type of influence exerts its specific effects, even upon those more advanced in years; and, —

Its results are more quickly realized than those of any other influences tending toward the same channel of ill health.

BASKET-MAKING.

An observation of females, varying in age from sixteen to forty, engaged in basket-making, — a labor requiring wonderful rapidity of manipulation, — showed, that, in half a dozen new operatives placed upon the work in a well-ventilated, light, and cheerful room, —

1. Five lost in weight in the first week appreciably; the remaining one, a slower person, apparently not at all.

2. The youngest lost the largest per cent of weight.

3. Two, one sixteen and another eighteen, experienced disturbance of the menstrual function in the first month of employ, though previously regular.

4. The slow person began to lose weight appreciably on the fourth week, when her motions had quickened.

5. The decrease in weight continued with all (though there was no diminution of appetite or general health specially noticeable) for from four to six weeks; when, the move-

ments of the digits having become more mechanical, it ceased, and the weight remained essentially unchanged for a few weeks, varying with individuals, from one to three, when in four of the six it increased perceptibly, in the other two slightly. The operatives of this department state, that a change in the shape of their work, requiring for a time more concentrated thought, will, if it occur at that juncture, effect sometimes a disturbance of the catamenial function. In all, familiarity with the work tends to remove the difficulty.

THE COUNTING OF MONEY, ETC.

The continuous counting of money or certain other articles, conducted as a regular employment, presents, perhaps, the purest type of manipulative celerity, co-operative with extreme mental concentration, known to investigators. It has, moreover, the especial characteristic that only to a very slight degree, if at all, can it be made "mechanical." It cannot be performed unconsciously, but demands constant vigilance and alert digital reciprocity.

Satisfied that a pursuit so entirely representing extreme mental concentration, with most rapid physical manipulation, could not fail of producing a marked effect upon such girls of "forming" age as should be employed therein, inquiry was made at the United States Treasury at Washington, in the "counting department" of which some thirty ladies are constantly employed in counting "currency." This counting is of pieces of one denomination at a time only ; i.e., a person counting "tens" counts tens only for the time being; and one upon "fifties" handles only pieces of that designation: hence the pieces, and not the amount, are counted, the number of pieces multiplied by the denomination, of course, giving the result in dollars and cents. The skill acquired in this department is truly wonderful, some of those employed counting millions of pieces per year. Let any one take a few hundred pieces of currency, and attempt to count them as rapidly as possible, and it will be found that not only is the manual movement exceedingly rapid, but that the mental concentration is most intense, monotonous, and unremitting; while the result attained, even at the utmost endeavor, is not very great. It will hence be readily understood, that in the constant employ at this occupation there must of necessity be a most exhausting draft upon the mental and physical forces. Exactly such is found to be the case; and this pursuit, which, it will be seen, combines, to a degree that no other we have considered does, the several special influences of mental depression, concentration, alertness, continued exercise, and monotony, exercises its deleterious power upon the periodicity of its followers in the way and with the rapidity that we should expect.

Miss ———, the lady longest in the employ of the department, and in charge of the "counting" (over thirteen years), states that, —

OBJECTIVE.

"The girls usually come into the work looking rosy and healthy; but they very soon grow pale-lipped and pale-cheeked, and soon begin to require more or less absence. When they first begin the work, they all sit very straight, and count very fast, although I always counsel them against the fast counting; for no one has ever yet undertaken it that did not break down, if young. Gradually they learn to count faster, but they cannot continue in the work but a short time. The sickness and absence become more frequent, and by and by they are obliged to leave altogether. We have those over fifty, and one of sixty years of age employed; *and they are the only ones, with perhaps a single exception, who do not seem to feel the effects.*"

Question. "What is the exception?" *Answer.* "We have a young lady who counts easily, and looks off her work more or less, and is not in general so closely confined to her work as the others, and does not seem to feel it as much as they."

Q. "Do you consider that she can do her work 'mechanically,' then?" *A.* "She thinks she can."

Q. "Do you?" *A.* "We do not find her work as correct."

Q. "You would hardly be willing to trust it?" *A.* "We do not."

Q. "Have you satisfied yourself of the way, the direction, in which this steady and concentrated labor acts upon your young ladies?" *A.* "They all suffer more or less from headaches, severe backaches, debility, and constipation, but all the younger ones, particularly, from too frequent and profuse return of their menses. I think this last the worst feature; for, as soon as that begins, they lose color, grow nervous and feeble, are often absent, and suffer along till they 'give up.'"

Q. "Are there any influences connected with the work other than those which, as we see, are part of it, that act badly on the employées?" *A.* "Our rooms are fearfully hot, — most unhealthily so, I think; and of course the stoop which a girl soon gets is bad, as well as her sitting so long in one position. No other unhealthy 'influences.'"

Q. "You consider, then, that the very character of the work is surely and rapidly prejudicial to the health of the young women engaged in it, and especially on account of their sex?" *A.* "Yes, I do; and they cannot remain it but a very short time. It told upon me severely when I began, and I was matured when I began; and, if I had been at the counting, I could not have remained."

The counting of "strands" of rattan, used in "cane-seating" furniture, etc., is an employment which, as carried on at Wakefield and Fitchburg, Mass., employs a large number of women and girls. The work consists in each of those engaged drawing rapidly and continuously from a large roll of tangled strands, just as received from the "hatcheling" machine, one or more of these strips, and straightening it, placing them on a peg upon the wall, so arranged that the strand length can be measured as it hangs; and subsequently counting them off into bundles, the latter part being performed with great rapidity. There is no aid to the counting except that each operative learns, in time, about how many her right hand will hold; for, as she holds the loose bundle of strands in her left, she transfers them, with a swift, sliding motion, under the thumb of the right, until the hand is full, thereby in time acquiring a general idea of about how many it would usually contain. The allied mental and physical demands of the process itself are closely similar to those of money-counting, but the labor has the additional exhaustive characteristic that it is performed standing.*

An inquiry among those engaged in this department, and into the factory record of those who have been so employed, establishes the following: —

Young girls of the forming period are not now put upon the work at all, it having been found that it was impossible for them to continue it long.

With those of more advanced age, the menopause is more or less affected, the gen-

---

* "The same causes of ill health, physical and mental, which obtain in many schools, and which to my mind are very efficient in mischief to the developing woman, are found, as we all know, in shops and factories, in constant operation, and in the most aggravated form. I consider those employments which require girls from twelve to twenty to stand at the counter or loom from eight to twelve hours a day, week in and week out, as little short of suicidal, *murderous* perhaps I should say. Table and nursery girls, in hotels and city houses, are notable subjects of menorrhagia, anæmia, chlorosis, and often of hysterical excitement or melancholia. These things are matters of experience to every physician, though hard to present in statistical form." — THEO. W. FISHER, M. D.: *Letter to author.*

eral disturbance being in the direction of menorrhagia, or profuse menstruation.

The more advanced toward matured adult life the individual, the better she is able to endure the hardship of the employ.

There is general suffering with those so engaged, from persistent headache, dropsical affections, and severe dyspepsia; while not infrequent uterine inflammations and displacement have come under my own knowledge among the operatives in this department.

Few have been able to follow it for any length of time, and these not continuously; the duration of employ being closely proportionate to the maturity of the individual.

A casual inquiry among stenographers has assured me, that, although a vocation admirably adapted in many of its features for the exercise of female ability, and embracing demands for the deft celerity, with the ready perception and appreciation of women; its requirements of concentration and nervous force are such, as well as considerable physical endurance, that women shrink from it, although the demand for skilled stenographers is daily greater. The United States census of 1870 shows that only *three* had thus far established themselves as such. One of the most expert of this class in the country gives it as his opinion, that " constant employ therein would inevitably break a young woman down in a short time." It certainly is significant, that an employment whose general characteristics, associations, and pecuniary return may be said to be so enticing to women should not have attracted to its ranks larger numbers, when the field is so wide. Were it not that its effects, and the difficulty of securing success therein without incurring them, have become recognized, it certainly would seem that its labors would have been far more widely adopted.

SEWING-MACHINE LABOR.

The several branches of industry hitherto considered have all been such as have their physical requirements principally met by the labor of the hands alone (except such involvement of pedal power as was embraced in standing, walking, etc.); but, in sewing-machine use, we have an employ calling into exercise the active service of the feet and lower limbs, which, as more closely allied to the organs involved in menstruation, and to a certain extent enjoying the same vascular system, may be considered as possessing a new relay of interest. While all the pursuits dwelt upon have been characterized by a greater or less degree of disadvantage in posture, in the use of the sewing-machine this disadvantage is rather aggravated than otherwise. There is no need to enlarge upon the extent of its use, or to state that the use of power-propelled machines does not fall under review; nor will it be necessary, in view of the exhaustive examinations of the subject by Guibout,[*] Decaisne,[†] Nichols,[‡] and others, to

---

[*] Paper before "Soc. Médicale des Hôpitaux."

[†] Ann. d'Hyg. Pub. 1870, 2d ser. vol. xxxvi.

[‡] Dr. A. H. Nichols, 3d Rep. Board of Health, Mass.

do more than adapt their findings to the place they properly hold in relation to the results we are considering.

While the investigations of Guibout are characterized, on the one hand, by an exaggeration of the injurious influences incident to sewing-machine use, and those of Decaisne, on the other hand, by a too slight regard for these influences (though his inquiries were extended), the more nearly trustworthy deductions of Dr. Nichols [*] establish a series of "conclusions" which expose a grave degree of harm. The comprehensive question asked by Dr. Nichols of his correspondents was, "Have you observed any injury to health from the use of sewing-machines used by foot-power? If so, please to send us all the information you may have on the subject."

Replies were received from one hundred and thirty-eight correspondents, representing one hundred and twenty towns in Massachusetts, and several in other States.

---

[*] Dr. A. H. Nichols, 3d Rep. Board of Health, Mass.

OBJECTIVE. 117

Eighty report more or less ill effects observed by them; the balance, giving negative or doubtful answers, were mainly from towns where the machines were used only in private families, etc. My own analysis of the published replies shows that sixty-nine physicians replied to the query. Of this number, forty-four answered in an emphatic manner, declaring the results to be undoubted upon the organs of menstruation and the function itself; four, only, held negative views; while the remainder assigned to the use other results indirectly operative to the same end.

I quote a few only, taken at random from the many unequivocal statements of these physicians as to the pernicious effects of this industry.

REPLIES FROM MASSACHUSETTS PHYSICIANS.

A. "Quite a number of cases, in which pain and lameness in the back and thighs, dyspepsia, leucorrhœa, vaginitis, and menorrhagia existed, I have attributed to their use."

B. "The most common disease I have seen is a

chronic form of ovaritis, which it is impossible to cure while the girl is at work."

C. "The use of the machine during menstruation is especially injurious. I have even known a case where a severe attack of ovaritis and retroflexion of the uterus followed its use during a single menstrual period."

D. "I think I have observed a greater tendency to dysmenorrhœa and other uterine troubles among those who use the sewing-machine for a living than among others."

E. "Cases of unmistakable injury, very frequent a few years ago, causing marked irregularities of the menstrual function, and their usual *sequelæ*. The almost universal introduction of steam-power has greatly diminished this class of cases."

F. "Constant and long-continued use of sewing-machines, moved by foot-power, tends to induce functional diseases of the uterus. Three girls working in the same shop ten hours daily, for two or three years, now suffer from dysmenorrhœa, from which they were formerly free."

Says a Boston physician[*] who for many years has given special attention to the gynæcological affections of women, —

---

[*] Horatio R. Storer, M.D., Lecture on Female Hygiene, before State Board of Health of California, p. 13.

"The sewing-machine, that compound of blessing and curse to woman, adds to the list of influences causative of disease, not only acting in several of the ways suggested, by the long-continued and constrained position and fatiguing of the pelvic muscles ; but in another, not generally sufficiently appreciated, by which a mental and dangerous disquietude is originated and enhanced by the unintentional auto-stupration."

Another well-known physician [*] of Boston writes : —

"I once observed many cases of debility, and pain in spine and side, with now and then menstrual disorders, in a shopful of sewing-machine girls, which ceased to exist when steam was applied."

OTHER PHYSICIANS.

A. "I have investigated quite a number of cases where diseases were produced by running sewing-machines by foot-power. Among these diseases, I have noticed several cases of lameness of limbs and back, menorrhagia, dysmenorrhœa, amenorrhœa, leucorrhœa, and displacements."

B. "I have no doubt whatever that this employ-

---

[*] Theo. W. Fisher, M.D.: Letter to the author.

ment among females is more powerful and efficient in the production of disease of various kinds in that sex than almost all other causes combined."

To these expressions of physicians, presumably as safe a criterion of the real results produced by the occupation as can be obtained, Dr. Nichols has added numerous varying experiences of the workwomen themselves, which, though not as harmonious or positive in their findings, are sufficiently so to make it certain that a grave degree of peculiar disturbance is recognized by them. The "conclusions" given by Dr. Nichols are: —

"That the illnesses which most frequently prevail among professional operatives (as distinguished from home operatives) making use of the treadle (foot-power) are, —

"(*a*) Indigestion, attributable to the unhealthy conditions in which they pursue their occupation, particularly the impure atmosphere of the workrooms, the sedentary employment, and want of open-air exercise.

"(*b*) Muscular pains, affecting the lower limbs and trunk, produced by the long-continued, frequent use of the muscles.

"(c) Diseases peculiar to women, aggravated by, rather than caused by, the plethoric condition of the pelvic organs, induced by this exercise.

"(d) General debility. By this is meant a state of physical deterioration and nervous prostration brought on by overwork."

Adding to these conclusions the single remark, that my own observations and review of the data given would indicate a classification of these influences upon female ill health as more decidedly "causative" than "aggravating," the belief may fairly be educed therefrom, that in the continued use of the sewing-machine by foot-power, there resides a source of special functional disturbance in women, which is extensive in its reach, and embraces overwork, often under bad sanitary surroundings, labor to which much of the monotony and unremitting character incident to most machine-work attaches, and muscular activity coupled with a considerable degree of mental concentration; this last being in an intermediate degree to that required by factory machinery, and that required by the telegraph instrument. The evidence of the direct influence of this species of employ upon the catamenial function is notably abundant, and raises the query, if the fact of pedal rather than manual muscular power as here involved is the real *cause* of a greater effect; or, whether the simpler methods of argument cause those affected (by localizing the energy in closer relation to the parts seen to be most influenced) to *infer* an injury that they would be slow to recognize when remote agents, as the hand, are active, and the brain must be summoned to greater participation to produce the effect. As an employment still enlisting the labors of large numbers of young women of the ages we are considering, notwithstanding the very considerable introduction of steam-power to its uses, it is well worthy the consideration of the economist and legislator; for from its ranks the offices of wife and mother are filled to no mean degree, few of the class continuing many years in the work, while those engaged therein are, as a rule,

OBJECTIVE.

of different fibre from those of factory labor, and do not like them raise up and perpetuate succeeding generations of employées for the same work.

We may fairly conclude, from the foregoing testimony and data from the various channels of industry, —

First, That a sure and swift result must follow to the immature female whenever she engages in an employ requiring mental and physical concentration and celerity.

Second, That the disturbance will be proportionate, in the rapidity of its advance and degree, to the degree of concentration, celerity, and continuity of employ.

Third, That its most active and most baleful effects will be upon the functions peculiar to the sex.

Whatsoever, therefore, in industry, exerts these influences (whose present and prospective and almost unending results we have pointed out), demands the exercise of all ingenuity, wisdom, and care, to secure its alleviation and removal. Certain of the employments of women include these evils from seeming present necessity; but it becomes the duty of all to direct their studious attention thereto, if perchance a relief may be found; while for other forms of employ only the false notions that exist need to be overthrown, to banish at least some of their attendant evils.

PART III.

SUGGESTIVE.

"The commonwealth is to take necessary measures for the protection of public health, and to secure society against whatever may be a public nuisance or a public peril." — MULFORD: *The Nation*, p. 286.

I HAVE intimated that the exactions of distorted views of life, the consequent disarrangement of economic adjustments, and woman's own mistaken ambitions, have inflicted upon her a position in industrial toil foreign to the true intent of her being. In brief, she must now labor for bread in the same field with men, and, so doing, falls short of, is outside, her true and highest possibilities and privileges. What, then, are these? and how may the designed condition, so far as industry is concerned, be brought about? Says Maudsley: * —

"Could we in imagination trace mankind backward along the path stretching through the ages, on which it has gone forward to its present height and complexity of emotion, and suppose each new emotional element to be given off at the spot where it was acquired, we should view a road along which the fragments of our high, special, and complex feeling were scattered, and should reach a starting-point of the primitive instincts of self preservation and propagation.

"In the first place, a proper regard to the physical nature of women means attention given, in their training, to their peculiar functions, and to their fore-ordained work as mothers and nurses of children. Whatever aspirations of an intellectual kind they may have, they cannot be relieved from the performance of those offices so long as it is thought necessary that mankind should continue on earth."

For woman is reserved, therefore, the distinctive glory and honor of the chief agency in the perpetuity, development, and training of her race. To a distinction so dignified, a

---

* Sex in Mind and Education, Henry Maudsley, M.D.

position so ennobling, the highest enthronement is fittingly to be accorded.

" Nothing," says Gaskell, * " would tend more to elevate the moral condition of the population than the restoration of woman to her proper social rank; nothing would exercise greater influence upon the form and growth of her offspring than her devotion to those womanly occupations which would render her a denizen of home. No great step can be made till she is snatched from unremitting toil, and made what nature meant she should be, — the centre of a system of social delights. Domestic avocations are those of her peculiar lot. The poor man who suffers his wife to work, separated from him and from home, is a bad calculator."

To bring woman to the position she should hold in the world's work, is hence but to recognize her, in the fullest sense, as the custodian and exponent of powers and principles of paramount importance, not only to the well-being, but to the very existence of the race. Sex, God-implanted, imperative for the very possibility of being, claims for

---

* Op. cit. p. 166.

itself more than ordinary recognition: it demands the most enlarged consideration. Woman, as we have seen, holds in industry a position inconsistent and incompatible with the coeval possession of her true plane.

To take things as they are, and without creating disaster in the machinery of society, to bring the female worker to the higher level of her intended vocation, is a problem not easy of solution, and yet is the one that it is all essential, if we are to retain our place and nation, should receive a not tardy demonstration. In the adaptation of educational systems to the physiological needs of the forming girl, the measures to be taken are few and obvious. To re-adjust industry on the same basis, and to the same ends, involves such an intricacy of detail, such an innovation of existing customs, and so entire an overthrow of the established order of things, that any movement in this direction must be exceedingly gradual, and attack only the edges of the great mass of error.

I may presume, therefore, only to offer a

few suggestions which aim at improvement of existing conditions in industry; hoping that in some degree I may have made bare, for the steel of more stalwart axemen, the roots and fibres that bind us to degeneracy and decay.

That for years to come, our girls of forming age will continue from necessity to enter the various lines of industry, there can be no doubt. And, so long as it is a necessity imposed by the duty of bearing the burden of self-support that else must fall unduly on others, the toil becomes a dignity; and, so long as it be honest, ennobles the laborer. Hence the dignity of labor is universal; and there is no rightful pride of superiority which one form may exercise over another, so long as the one engaged in is the best for which the individual is fitted, for the result to herself and society. The book-keeper trained to that employ has no right of superiority over the sewing-machine girl trained to that work, by virtue of the more distinctively mental character of her pursuit. But there is a comparison that may rightfully be, and should be drawn, between these employments of women; and it is based solely on their respective effects on the health of the operative. It is to such a distinction, as affecting wages, hours, and the persistence of labor of employées, that we look for a measure of good to the working-girl. A scientific gradation of pursuits as to their salubrity or non-salubrity, their physiological effects, will sooner or later be effected, and govern, to a great degree, the participation therein of the forming female. The influences * affecting moral conditions in various

---

* While these last pages have been going through the press, I have received a letter from a widely-known physician in one of the large manufacturing cities of this State; in which, speaking of the evil effects of moral and physical disregard in the want of privies, or the bad location thereof, he says, "A trip to L—— to examine the water-closets of the workshops of this place would pay, or, rather, to see the general lack of all convenience in the shops for women and girls. I am satisfied that a very large proportion of disease in our L—— female population is due to the fact that so few facilities are afforded women to attend to calls of nature.

classes of employ, as inseparable from definite physical and physico-moral effects on those employed therein, will, also, undoubtedly come in for a much-needed share of consideration.

It has not been difficult to discover and point out the errors and evils that attend upon the several forms of employ, and that operate against the health, happiness, and usefulness of women. To suggest the remedies for these is obviously a matter of no small moment, and not easy of accomplishment.

As there are basis principles of health, which are affected, as we have seen, by these conditions of employ, so are there basis prin-

"I am equally satisfied, from the fact, that in shops where a water-closet is so exposed that women must be seen by all the men when they enter, that that alone has a bad moral influence upon them. I *know* it; and in a conversation I had in my office to-day, with a girl of eighteen, who suffered severely from constipation, and inflammation of the bladder (that being her usual habit), she gave as a cause, that, in her shop, the men could see every girl that visited the closet, and that therefore none but the *bad* girls would go."

ciples of error which lie at the root of all branches of wrong.

I believe that the grave mistakes of our labor system, as affecting the class of females considered, are, —

First, That we employ those therein whose years absolutely prohibit their being employed at labor *at all*.

Second, That their hours of labor are too long; and, —

Third, That we sadly neglect the measures that are adaptable to insure a correct sanitary condition of our operatives during their labor.

Under one or the other of these cardinal forms of error, all the specific evils of different occupations or circumstances will arrange themselves.

No child or young person of *either* sex, under the age of fifteen years, should ever be engaged in any form of industrial employ necessitating absence from school, or a draft on vital energy. The normal position of those of that age is in the work of education ; and, until this is recognized, the nation and individuals must suffer present and future loss, — loss of bodily vigor, without which a nation must die; loss of knowledge, which is power to upbuild, to keep, to develop; loss in the higher values that belong to the nobler parts of our being, and that cannot expand in a soul or body dwarfed and exhausted by the gross demands of purely animal existence.

But it is objected, it can be clearly shown in this Commonwealth, that while it is true, that the money in savings banks, to a considerable extent, belongs to laboring people, little of it would be there if it were not for the labor of women and children, the wives and offspring of laboring men ; indeed, that, without their assisting labor, it is proved that the average laborer could not make the ends of the year meet. Granted ; and yet my proposition is nevertheless of full force, and for two reasons : —

First, Because it is plain that there is an error in that price and form of labor that will not permit a man to support his family in comfort without drawing on the vital powers of those to whom we must look to make his place good, and to not only carry on, but improve upon, the work of society.

Second, Because we can never afford to set a price upon body and soul; and any barter of strength, happiness, and knowledge, for mere money-return, is an exchange that will surely rob us in the long-run.

Is it true, as scientists * tell us, that there is a progressive decline and deterioration in the mental vigor and physical stability of our people? We have to thank for it these errors that exhaust the life of the fathers and mothers of coming generations, to convert it

---

* "That there has been a decided change in female organization in New England within fifty or a hundred years, there can be no question. Formerly there was more muscle, a larger frame, greater fulness of form, and a better development of all those organs that are classed under the sanguine and lymphatic temperaments. The brain and nervous system relatively were not especially predominant; neither were they taxed continuously or excessively above any other class of organs." — NATHAN ALLEN, M.D.: *Medical Problems of the Day*, p. 78.

by a base alchemy into present gold, — a gold that by and by, like that of the Phrygian king, will be all there is to offer as bread, as homes, as armies, as thought-power, and as happiness.

The hours of labor are too long, — not too long to earn a living in, for they barely suffice, as things now stand, for the purpose; but too long for the proper physical good, mental culture, and moral growth of those involved. The proper physical good is especially our concern. If the co-operative system of labor ever reaches a general result as favorable as that its individual successes would warrant a hope of, I believe there may then be both time and an inclination (not existing at its best in a worn body and tired mind) to regard those questions of personal cleanliness, diet, clothing, hygienic surroundings, and physical development, now so sadly disregarded by the working-classes, wherever found. An hour more in the morning for the young and forming female (and that is where it may be most advantageously gained, as all labor investigators agree) would save the necessity of ill-cooked, hurriedly-eaten, badly-digested breakfasts (made on hurriedly-prepared food, in which tea holds a prominent place), unwashed faces, neglect of nature's calls, hurried passage to the place of employ, and a disturbed, dissatisfied, and fermenting body and mind, stomach and brain. Get a right conception and *adoption* of the true relation of these things into the mind and lives of working-people, and half the complaints that now arise, like those from the Israelites in the desert, will cease, as did theirs, with the right appreciation of the manna from heaven.

Remedy these ills, and thereby elevate the intrinsic character of working-girls, and a large part of the invidious social distinction made between brain-labor and hand-labor, against the latter, will die a natural death.

An advanced intelligence and humanity is yet to recognize, moreover, the adaptation not only of the right strength, but the right hours of employ, at the various processes of labor. There are occupations at which a Hercules has no right to labor a full day, and they should be graded as such, and others in proportion; the hours of labor being adjusted for the labor, just as the strength of the individual should be adapted to it.

It is not sought to raise a nation of effeminates or *dilettanti;* nor do we wish, on the other hand, to make the land a hospital for worn-out, debilitated, dyspeptic, chlorotic, anæmic, unsexed men and women. Shorter hours of labor, better improved, on better systems of the divisions of profits, may be, to some degree at least, an antidote.

We sadly neglect the measures that are adaptable to insure a correct sanitary condition of our operatives during their labor. Of this the proof is in every workshop, salesroom, and office in the land. Every occupation proves it, and the diseases and mortality registers make it indisputable. What can be done to remedy this general neglect, and what to meet, with special preventives, the specific dangers of definite occupations? There can be but two ways in which either the general or the detailed ills of this nature can be met. They are, the diffusion of sound intelligence bearing thereon, and the enactment and enforcement of efficient repressing law. The dissemination of intelligence to a degree that shall cause sex to be recognized in labor; a fitness of things in the apportionment of occupations, both as to strength and time; that shall convince legislators of the necessity of laws, and their enforcement in these directions; that shall demonstrate to the employer the certainty that every draft he makes upon the vital forces of by and by, must be paid out of his children's pockets and their lives, — *such* a dissemination is at once the most powerful and the slowest-growing of influences. Much of it, however, must exist before the second influence — legislation and its execution — can be established. So long as men are prone to consult their own selfish interests, so long as the present is a greater reality than the future in the eyes of men; the simple *existence*, in partial recognition, of principles which, however vital they may be, are found to be at variance with men's interests, or to deal largely with the future, will not be sufficient to command the respect they intrinsically demand. It becomes necessary that the minds that do recognize what other minds would recognize but for their blinds of self-interest and distance, must bring into operative force the principles that should prevail; and this can be only through the medium of law. *

---

* Says Dr. Jarvis, "Can government aid in improving human life? Is there room here in the field of human life for governmental co-operation, as well as in the agricultural field of vegetable and animal life? It is powerful there: it is not powerless, and need not be ineffective, here. The power of government is threefold, and is executed in a triple way. It is mandatory, and says, Thou shalt, and thou shalt not. It is permissive, and grants privileges. It is advisory, instructive, and encouraging. It teaches the people their best interests, and points the way of gaining them." — *Polit. Econ. of Health*, Op. cit. p. 263.

It is hence essential, that such enactments should be made and prosecuted as shall best establish the condition of things that should be; and it is to such well-considered and efficient enactments that we must look for the prevention of much that now affects most unfavorably the condition of working-people, and especially women and children. Provision for the due inspection of, and inquiry into, the real conditions of labor, is naturally indicated as the initial desideratum of such law, and in this Commonwealth is especially necessary.

What is needed is the existence of inspectors of labor concomitants, with laws sufficiently regulative of those conditions, and power in the inspectors acting under those laws to maintain them as they should be. But inasmuch as the inspector, without law to establish what is evil and what good, is useless, though with it most potent, the *law* becomes the chief agent in the work of reform; and it is to the wise creation and the subsequent execution of these laws that we must look for an improvement.

Says Dr. Jarvis,[*] —

"In as far as human life is more important than all financial interests, and, even in the financial view, the creative power of human force is more valuable than all created capital, this cardinal interest of the people, individually and collectively, should take precedence of all other provisions in all legislation. Every law, grant, or privilege from the legislature should have this invariable condition: that human health, strength, or comfort should in no manner or degree be impaired or vitiated thereby.

To frame laws to meet the demands of the principles I have recognized, under all their varying conditions, is not a task for this space, or one to be readily accomplished; but we may fairly consider, in brief, some of the ends it is specially desirable should receive the appreciation of the public in general, and the employer in particular, and, it is to be hoped, will eventually find their recognition in law. It is believed, —

That the employment at labor of any girl

---

[*] Op. cit. p. 371.

under fifteen years of age should not be allowed.*

That the employment of girls of other ages — and women generally — at employments unsuited to their sex should not be suffered (such employments being determined by a council of salubrity, in France, composed of those most eminently fit for their high commission).†

That, in such employments as women should be admitted to, they should be permitted a "periodical absence," without pecuniary loss, for such time as might be just and necessary.

That in employments where women should be admitted, and which require high degrees of mental concentration, with physical energy, additional vacations of sufficient extent should be the right of the employée.

---

* Prof. Clarke has summed it up tersely when he says, "If excessive labor, either mental or physical, is imposed upon children, male or female, their development will in some way be checked." — *Op. cit.* p. 41.

† See appendix.

That, in all employments, it should be obligatory upon the employer to conduct the processes of the occupation under the most advantageous conditions to health, and to secure all improvements in this regard that may become approved.

That in all larger manufactories (of over certain numbers of employées) there should be special sanitary supervision at the expense of the proprietors.

That there should be a well-established examination and certification of all employés, male and female, proposing to engage in any deleterious or burdensome employ, — only those being certified who are found in the possession of health not to be unduly impaired thereby, and only such to be employed as are certified.

To the clause which provides, that in all employments it should be obligatory upon the employer to conduct the processes of the occupation under the most advantageous conditions to health, etc., I desire to direct attention. To improve is the possibility of the present; to re-establish may be the work of centuries. We may and should, therefore, prosecute the improvement at once and assiduously. Dr. Clarke has suggested, that " the keen eye and rapid hand of gain, of what Jouffroy calls self-interest well understood, is sometimes quicker than the brain and will of philanthropy to discern and inaugurate reform." He says, —

" There is an establishment in Boston, owned and carried on by a man, in which ten or a dozen girls are constantly employed. Each of them is given, and is required to take, a vacation of three days every fourth week. It is scarcely necessary to say, that their sanitary condition is exceptionally good, and that the aggregate yearly amount of work which the owner obtains is greater than when persistent attendance and labor was required."

Unfortunately for woman and the race, few such cases of wise regard exist with employers; but it is precisely this condition of things that ought to exist, and become not the exception, but the unvarying custom. If the same consideration for employées were everywhere exhibited as that shown by the Blackstone Mill at Blackstone, which has provided bath-rooms for its operatives, or the Hamilton Mills at Lowell, which have put in operation a new form of shuttle, by which the dangers incident to the old way of sucking the thread through in filling the shuttle are removed, the employers, woman, and the race, would be greatly the gainers.

Improved apparatus and less injurious processes, ventilation, the instant removal of dust from dust-producing machinery, the utilization of steam (now injuriously wasted in " weave-rooms ") in heating water for baths, proper kinds, conditions, and seclusion of privies, warm dressing-rooms for girls at mills, etc., where wet clothing, may be changed, alternation of labors when processes are specially exacting, seats for girls in stores, and better opportunities for food, such as are to be obtained through " cooking-depots," " Holly-tree inns," — etc., all are agencies, which, with many others that might yet be enumerated, will powerfully act for the amelioration of the condition of the working female of whatever age, but have especial powers of good for the forming girl.

The walls of the factories at Wakefield and other places, blackened by the foul vapors escaping from their privies, attest the character of the atmosphere the operatives breathe. The foul condition and exposed location of these privies have been already shown. Wet floors, draughty rooms, and severe toil, so widely the rule in manufacturing establishments, have forced upon many a working girl an overthrow of her special forces, that ended in clouded intellect, broken health, and early death.

It behooves the state, therefore, to stand, *first*, as the legal protector of its most weighty interests, its perpetuity and progress; and, *second*, as the patron and promoter of whatever will aid therein. It has been deemed wise to stimulate, from time to time, special thought and inventive genius in

SUGGESTIVE. 147

aid of agricultural * or commercial interests, by the promise of large pecuniary rewards. What more legimate, or more desirable, than that the commonwealth should use every spur to bring to the lives and health of its inhabitants every device by which they may be additionally secured or promoted? If it be advisable to offer large rewards to him who shall discover the prevention of rot in the potato (an article of food of comparatively small value, physiologically considered), and to bestow a prize of due proportion for " the

---

* "It is shown by the statistical tables of Continental Europe, that the annual human increase depends upon the agricultural product of it; and so well is this established, that, in countries where the army is made up by the conscription of a certain proportion of the population, it has been found, that not only the number to be had can, with a fair chance of accuracy, be estimated from the state of the market eighteen to twenty years previously, but even the average standard height of the men furnished." — KREPP: *The Sewage Question*, p. 9.

If this be so, is it not a rational thing, that powers fully as depletory and devitalizing as scarcity of food, viz., the inimical forces against the health of woman, should have an equally untoward effect against the vigor and numbers of a nation?

best essay on the building of roads," how much more so for the creation of agencies that shall lessen the dangers of dust in factories, of injury from machinery, of fatiguing labor at the sewing-machine, the telegraph-instrument, and the type-case, and free from their baleful force the foul vapors of our noxious trades! In nothing can the state more surely seek its riches; for he who thinks must accept the precept of Emerson, that "the first wealth is health."

That the worker herself may, by the exercise of recognized precautions, by personal attention to, or avoidance of, conditions unfavorable to health, and the cultivation of personal habits that aid the promotion thereof, do much to lessen the evil influences of labor, there can be no doubt.

So far as she sympathizes in, and gives aid to, the effort that a comparatively few of her sex have for some years persistently urged with a zeal worthy of a better cause, — for the *competitive* relation as between her and man in industry, — she countenances an

SUGGESTIVE.

error. It is an error whose one certain effect is, to keep her in an abnormal condition, *beneath* her rights, and *under* her opportunities. The thoughtful ones of her sex recognize this. Says Dr. Frances Emily White,* —

"When we look around upon the great industries of life, — mining, engineering, manufacturing, commerce, and the rest, — and consider how little direct agency woman has had in bringing them to their present stage of progress, we are compelled to believe, that she must not look toward direct competition with man for the best unfolding of her powers; but rather, while continuing to supplement him, as he does her, in the varied interests of their common life, that her future progress, as in the past, will consist mainly in the development of a higher character of womanhood, through the selection and consequent intension of those traits peculiar to her own sex."

Says Van de Warker,† —

"This effort of woman to invade all the higher forms of labor is a force battling with the established order of sexual relation."

---

* FRANCES E. WHITE, M.D.: *Woman's Place in Nature, Popular Science Monthly*, January, 1875, p. 301.

† Op. cit. p. 470.

Dr. Allen has said,* —

"In all the situations and pursuits of life, the Almighty has established bounds or limitations beyond which woman cannot go without defeating the primary objects of her creation : maternity is the primary law of her creation."

Says Dr. Maudsley,† —

"When we thus look the matter honestly in the face, it would seem plain, that women are marked out by nature for very different offices in life from those of men, and that the healthy performance of her special functions renders it improbable she will succeed, and unwise for her to persevere, in running over the same course at the same pace with him. For such a race she is certainly weighted unfairly. Nor is it a sufficient reply to this argument, to allege, as is sometimes done, that there are many women who have not the opportunity of getting married, or who do not aspire to bear children; for whether they care to be mothers, or not, they cannot dispense with those physiological functions of their nature that have reference to that aim, however much they might wish it; and they cannot disregard them in the labor of life without injury to their health."

---

* Nathan Allen, M.D., op. cit. p. 41.
† Sex in Mind and Education, p. 30.

The weight of evidence that may be presumed to be worthy of confidence and consideration would seem to leave no doubt that the normal, the God-appointed work of woman, wherein lie her full equality, her peerage, her glory, and her power, is that of the home and the mother, the rearer, the trainer, the blessing of man.

To the " noble army of martyrs," the tens of thousands of working-women, of all ages, in America to-day, who patiently and hopefully toil on year by year, under the abnormal burdens a disjointed and unreflective society imposes, I pay the tribute of my earnest sympathy, my admiration, and my humble effort. I am assured, that, out of the labyrinth of perplexity that has entangled the question of woman's rights, there will sooner or later be evolved this certainty: that the highest moral and physical well-being of a race demands that there shall be nothing in its conditions of life and labor that shall injure the richness and purity of the chief source whence its existence and its best influences come.

When a senator of one of the most rugged States of our cold north-east was asked the most valuable product of his section, he replied with unction, "Men, sir, men!" Cornelia's jewels are still the wealth of a woman and a state. The significance of Penelope's virtue is yet vital. For her right to rise from the ills that assail her sex in industry, her right to retain, through present enforced toil, her titles to future dignity and happiness, I make this plea for the working-girl.

For woman's best is unbegun, her advent yet to come.

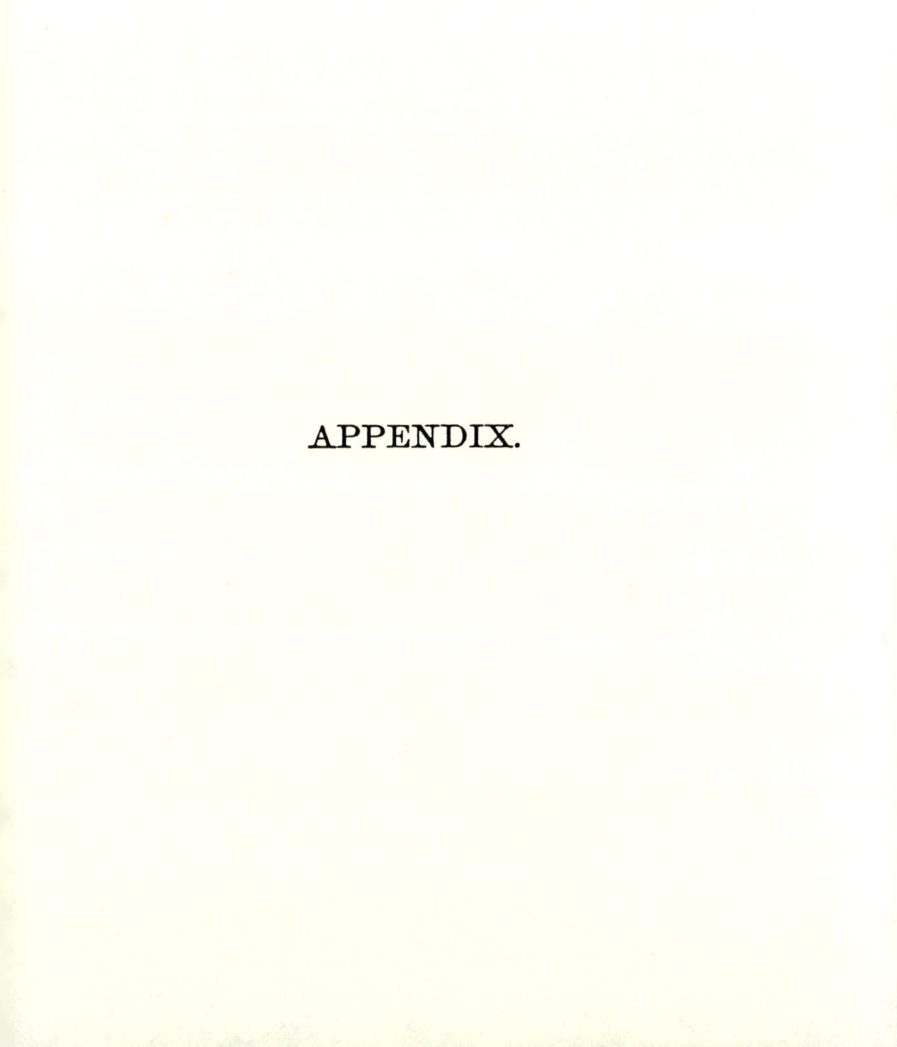

APPENDIX.

APPENDIX.

I.

THE following are the views of the celebrated M. Parent Duchalet of Paris as to the requirement of such a Council of Salubrity as I have referred to.

"It is generally thought in the world, that the medical knowledge acquired in the schools is all that is necessary to become a useful member of the council. The greater part of medical men themselves share this opinion ; and, on the strength of some precepts they have collected from books on health and professions, they think themselves sufficiently instructed to decide on the instant the gravest questions, which can only be resolved by special studies.

"A man may have exhausted medical literature ; he may be an excellent practitioner at the sick-bed, a learned physician, a clever and eloquent professor; but all these acquirements, taken in themselves, are nearly useless in a 'Conseil de Salubrité' like that of Paris ; and, if an occasion presents itself to make use of them, a very small number of persons suffice to apply them. To be really useful in the council, it is necessary to have an extended knowledge of natural philosophy, of the constitution of the soil on which the state or city stands, and of the geology of neighboring regions; it is necessary, above all, to know with exactness the action which trades may have on the health of those who exerçise them, and the much more important action of manufactories of every species on plants, on men congregated in towns, and on animals. This knowledge, so important, of the action of trades and manufactories, is not to be acquired by ordinary study, or in the silence of the cabinet. It is not to be obtained without positive notions on the arts, and on the greater part of the processes peculiar to each trade. It requires habit, and the frequenting of the places of work. In this particular, more even than in medicine, books are not a substitute for practice ; and, if there exist works on this subject, they are more likely to mislead than enlighten.

" From what has been said, the necessity will be evident, to introduce into the council those physicians who have made health, and particularly the public health, a special study ; and to join with them chemists, and, above all, manufacturing chemists : because what would many of those persons, whose life has been passed in hospitals and the exclusive study of medicine, be before a steam-engine ? It is clear that

APPENDIX.

they would often be deceived by those adroit and skilful manufacturers who would have an interest in concealing the truth."

II.

Since putting these sheets to press I have received the following from a lady operator with whom I had held conversation as to the special effects of telegraphy : —

BOSTON, Feb. 28, 1875.

DEAR SIR, — Pardon my delay, but I was obliged to wait some time to hear from the friend I mentioned. I find her views are similar to my own, and have nothing new to offer.

I made inquiries of the ladies employed in my room, as you requested; and all, with one exception, declared the business had no damaging effect upon the menstrual function: in *that* respect they have experienced no change since they entered the business. Take it as a whole, I believe telegraphy exerts no unfavorable influence in that direction, although it would seem to be a natural result on account of the nervousness inseparable from the business. Those I have consulted say every other function will be affected *except* the menstrual.

It is certainly true, that the business impairs the health of operators who work steadily, and they begin to run down in a year or so. Constipation is one great evil, and a general weariness. There is a constant strain upon the nerves and brain that is not required in other business; and yet our work has many advantages over other branches. Sitting so much is bad, but preferable to *standing* in a store from morning to night.

With a little rest now and then, or, at least, a *long* vacation once a year, I think the ladies would get along very well. Of course every one would *prefer* to rest at certain times; but, if women *must* work, I don't know but telegraphy is as healthy as any other business.

Respectfully Yours, ─────

It is to be said, in comment on the above, that in the office in question there is no operator under twenty, and that a careful inquiry has established the fact, that though this is the case, besides the disturbances spoken of above, two at least are sufferers from dysmenorrhea, and two from occasional menorrhagia which always improves on taking a vacation.

TITLES IN THIS SERIES

1 *Children's Hospitals in the Progressive Era: Two Investigations of Substandard Conditions*. David J. and Sheila M. Rothman, eds. New York, 1986
2 *The Consumer's League of New York: Behind the Scenes of Women's Work, Three Reports*. David J. and Sheila M. Rothman, eds. New York, 1986
3 *The Dangers of Education: Sexism and the Origins of Women's Colleges, An Anthology of Nineteenth Century Sources*. David J. and Sheila M. Rothman, eds. New York, 1986
4 *Divorce: The First Debates, A Collection of Articles*. David J. and Sheila M. Rothman, eds. New York, 1986
5 *Low Wages and Great Sins: Two Antebellum American Views on Prostitution and the Working Girl*. David J. and Sheila M. Rothman, eds. New York, 1986
6 *Maternal Mortality in New York City and Philadelphia, 1931–1933, Two Studies*. David J. and Sheila M. Rothman, eds. New York, 1986
7 *National Congress of Mothers, the First Conventions, 1897–1899*. David J. and Sheila M. Rothman, eds. New York, 1986
8 *The Origins of Adoption, Two Reports*. David J. and Sheila M. Rothman, eds. New York, 1986

9   *The Origins of Day Care: Selections from the Conferences on Day Nurseries, 1893–1925*. David J. and Sheila M. Rothman, eds. New York, 1986

10 *Risks for the Single Woman in the City, An Anthology of Studies by Late Nineteenth-Century Reformers*. David J. and Sheila M. Rothman, eds. New York, 1986

11 *Saving Babies: Children's Bureau Studies of Infant Mortality, 1913–1917*. David J. and Sheila M. Rothman, eds. New York, 1986

12 *The Sheppard-Towner Act, the Record of the Hearings*. David J. and Sheila M. Rothman, eds. New York, 1986

13 *Women in Prison, 1834–1928, An Anthology of Pamphlets from the Progressive Movement*. David J. and Sheila M. Rothman, eds. New York, 1986

14 Azel Ames, Jr., *Sex in Industry: A Plea for the Working Girl*, Boston, 1875

15 Robert South Barrett, *The Care of the Unmarried Mother*, Alexandria, 1929

16 Elizabeth Blackwell, M.D., *The Laws of Life, with Special Reference to the Physical Education of Girls*, New York, 1852

17 Alida C. Bower and Ruth S. Bloodgood, *Institutional Treatment of Delinquent Boys*, Washington, D.C., 1935–36

18 New York Assembly, *The Girls of the Department Store*, New York, 1895

19 Committee on the Infant and Preschool Child, *Nursery Education*, New York, 1931

20 Robert Latou Dickinson and Lura Beam, *The Single Woman: A Medical Study in Sex Education*, Baltimore, 1934

21 G. V. Hamilton, M.D., *A Research in Marriage*, New York, 1929

22 Elizabeth Harrison, *A Study of Child Nature from the Kindergarten Standpoint*, Chicago, 1909

23 Orie Latham Hatcher, *Rural Girls in the City for Work*, Richmond, 1930
24 William Healy, Augusta F. Bronner, et al., *Reconstructing Behavior in Youth*, New York, 1929
25 Henry H. Hibbs, Jr., *Infant Mortality: Its Relation to Social and Industrial Conditions*, New York, 1916
26 *The Juvenile Court Record*, Chicago, 1900, 1901
27 Mary A. Livermore, *What Shall We Do With Our Daughters?* Boston, 1883
28 *Massachusetts Society for the Prevention of Cruelty to Children: First Ten Annual Reports*, Boston, 1882
29 Maude E. Miner, *Slavery of Prostitution: A Plea for Emancipation*, New York, 1916
30 Maud Nathan, *The Story of an Epoch-Making Movement*, New York, 1926
31 National Florence Crittenton Mission, *Fourteen Years' Work Among "Erring Girls,"* Washington, D.C., 1897
32 New York Milk Committee, *Reducing Infant Mortality in the Ten Largest Cities in the United States*, New York, 1912
33 James Orton, ed., *The Liberal Education of Women: The Demand and the Method*, New York, 1873
34 Margaret Reeves, *Training Schools for Delinquent Girls*, New York, 1929
35 Ben L. Reitman, M.D., *The Second Oldest Profession*, New York, 1931
36 John Dale Russell and Associates, *Vocational Education*, Washington, D.C., 1938
37 William H. Slingerland, *Child Welfare Work in California*, New York, 1916
38 William H. Slingerland, *Child Welfare Work in Pennsylvania*, New York, 1917
39 *Documents Relative to the House of Refuge, Instituted by the Society for the Reformation of Juvenile Delinquents in the City of New York, in 1824*, New York, 1832

40 George S. Stevenson, M.D., and Geddes Smith, *Child Guidance Clinics*, New York, 1934

41 Henry Winfred Thurston, *Delinquency and Spare Time*, New York, 1918

42 U.S. National Commission on Law Observance and Enforcement, *Report on Penal Institutions, Probation and Parole*, Washington, D.C., 1931

43 Miriam Van Waters, *Parents on Probation*, 1927

44 Ira S. Wile, M.D., *The Sex Life of the Unmarried Adult*, New York, 1934

45 Helen Leland Witmer, *Psychiatric Clinics for Children*, New York, 1940

46 Young Women's Christian Association, *First Ten Annual Reports, 1871–1880*, New York, 1871–1880